# THE BEST IS
# YET TO COME...

# THE BEST IS YET TO COME...

## Saundra Kiczenski

Liberty Hill Publishing

Liberty Hill Publishing
2301 Lucien Way #415
Maitland, FL 32751
407.339.4217
www.libertyhillpublishing.com

Paperback ISBN-13: 978-1-6628-3832-3
Ebook ISBN-13: 978-1-6628-3833-0

# Table of Contents

— ★ —

# Introduction

———— ★ ————

My name is Saundra Kiczenski. I am not an author. I am just an ordinary citizen that started following politics in June 2015, soon after Donald Trump announced he was running for president of the United States. As a result, I traveled to fifty-six Donald Trump rallies from December 21, 2015, through January 6, 2021.

In this book, I will describe my experiences at the rallies and highlight some of what happened in the news cycle during these times. Toward the end of the book, I will discuss how I became a victim of a hit piece.

So, sit back, relax, and let's take a trip down memory lane.

# Chapter 1

## June 2016 to December 2016

———— ★ ————

I was never one to follow politics, and I watched very little news, but in the summer of June 16, 2015, that all changed for me. Donald Trump announced his candidacy for president of the United States in the 2016 election at Trump Tower in New York City. As time went by, this event was better known as "the famous escalator ride." I was not there, nor did I see this on television while it happened.

As some time went by, I heard about his announcement on the news. It was stated that his forty-five-minute campaign announcement speech was the longest of the major party candidates. I decided I would watch his speech online to see what he had to say.

I was impressed with his speech, as he was for "the people." He said what he was thinking right out loud, which was great. I liked that he would self-fund his presidential campaign and would not be taking money from lobbyists or donors.

A total of seventeen major candidates entered the race, which was the largest presidential field for any political party in American history. I listened to what the other candidates had to say, but they weren't as exciting as Donald Trump.

By now, it was August 2015, and I still remember saying, "I'm going to join that Trump train," and that's exactly what I did.

I had read online that there was a Trump rally in Grand Rapids at the DeltaPlex on December 21, 2015. I had never been to a political rally and had no idea what to expect. I didn't realize at the time that the previous rallies were viewable online. I decided to go.

I arrived at the DeltaPlex around noon. At this time, there was no one in line. I decided to go to the Big Boy for lunch and get in line a bit later. I arrived back to the DeltaPlex around 3:00 p.m. By this time, there was a line of people, and it was raining. I purchased my first Donald Trump souvenirs before going inside.

Just inside the door, they had the metal detectors set up. After going through those, the choice was to stand on the floor or take a seat. The capacity of this venue was 6200, and there was not an empty seat in the house. I chose to stand and was about ten rows from the stage. I noticed a lot of media had set up in the back area.

This was a Merry Christmas rally, so Christmas music played before the start of the rally. When Donald Trump came out, the place went wild. "Trump! Trump! Trump!" they cheered. Some protestors would pop up and would be escorted away immediately. The crowd yelled, "USA! USA! USA!" It was an amazing rally with so much energy.

At one point, Donald Trump asked the media to move the cameras to show the crowd, and I believe this was the first rally where they actually moved them, but that was very rare. I had taken in my first rally and thought, "When can I go again?"

In January 2016, I printed the 2016 primary schedule. This was a great way to follow the upcoming primaries. I had never followed the primaries in the past. and this was fun. It was a real learning experience. I learned that there were 2,340 delegates available, and the winner needed 1,237.

First was the Iowa caucus on February 1, 2016. Ted Cruz took the lead with eight delegates. During this time, the Ted Cruz campaign had left messages for supporters stating that Ben Carson had quit the race, even though he had not. He later apologized for doing so.

The primary in Michigan took place on March 8, 2016. Donald Trump announced that he would do a rally on March 3, 2016.

## Rally #2 – Cadillac, Michigan 3/4/2016

On March 3, 2016, I headed to Cadillac, Michigan. I arrived at the Wexford Center at around 10:30 a.m. Upon arrival, I looked inside to see that it was a small gym. I was told that bleachers would be set up to hold 1800, and there would also be a large area to stand.

I checked into the Holiday Inn since the rally was the next day. The Big Boy was close by, so I had my dinner there. At 5:20 a.m., cars lined up at the closed gate. They opened the gate at 7:15 a.m. for parking, and the doors opened at 10:30 a.m. It was stated that there were 3,500 people inside and 3,000 people outside. This rally started at 2:00 p.m., a bit of a late start, as Donald Trump had to land the plane elsewhere and motorcade in.

Since I was there early, I was able to get right at the front on the floor area. I discovered that this was a good spot because after the rally, Trump would sign autographs and take pictures for the people on the rope line. This was an exciting time, as you could get an autograph and shake his hand.

By the time Trump got to me, he paused for a minute, then he said, "Are you going to vote?" I told him that I had already voted by absentee ballot. Then he asked, "How are we doing in Michigan?" I said, "I think we are doing good." He said, "I think we're in good shape." During this time, I shook his hand, and he signed a small book I had brought with me that was called *50 Reasons to Vote for Donald Trump*.

I had been closely watching the delegate count as each primary took place. The Michigan primary was on March 8, 2016. Donald Trump received twenty-five delegates, with Cruz and Kasich at seventeen delegates. Donald Trump was right in that he took Michigan.

By March 2016, Donald Trump did a lot of campaign rallies. There were many times he would do several in a day. He received many views online, and the best network for coverage of these was Right Side Broadcasting Network (RSBN).

The Donald Trump rally in Fountain Hills, Arizona, on March 19, 2016, caught my attention. I waited to watch this one on television, but it was delayed. They showed highlights of what happened in the surrounding area. It was stated that dozens of protesters tried to stop the Trump rally, causing a dangerous traffic jam, according to the Maricopa County Sheriff's Office. During the rally, it was announced that protesters had chained themselves to cars, and three of them were arrested.

The Wisconsin primary was scheduled for April 5, 2016. Donald Trump announced some campaign rallies in Wisconsin. The first one was Janesville, Wisconsin, which was down by Milwaukee. I decided to travel to the rally in Appleton, Wisconsin, on March 30, 2016.

## Rally #3 – Appleton, Wisconsin 3/30/2016

I drove to Appleton, Wisconsin, the day before the rally. I arrived there at 10:15 a.m. Later in the day, I checked out the venue. When I arrived, they were setting up nice, cushioned chairs; there were approximately 1,000 seats available. They already had a large sign in place that said, "Line for Trump Presentation Starts Here." I noticed the first few in line would be under an awning and could also sit on a ledge. I decided to get there at 3:30 a.m. No one was there yet, but some people started arriving by 4:00 a.m., and I met some nice people at this rally.

By 10:00 a.m., the line was very long. Thousands of people did not get in. We had to go through a large lobby area to enter a security check area. We were in a very large conference room. I had a good seat for this one, which was front-row center. While we waited in line, someone bought meatballs subs for the people in the front of the line.

This was a great rally, as it was my first time hearing Trump recite The Snake poem in person. At the end of the rally, he did pictures and autographs for the front row. At this rally, I got the *Art of the Deal* book signed, which I had brought with me to read while I waited in line outside of the venue.

## Rally #4 – Rothschild, Wisconsin 4/2/2016

The rally in Rothschild, Wisconsin, was held at the Central Wisconsin Convention and Expo Center on April 2,

2016, at 3:00 p.m. This was ninety-eight miles west of Appleton. At this venue, a Bear Hunters' Convention was also held. I got to the lot early in the morning; some other cars were also there. We sat chairs up right at the entrance to the venue. The line for this one was right along a strip mall. This venue had 1,200 seats and 600 standing. The line to get in was very long, and many did not get in. I was thankful to have front-row center again. It was a very enthusiastic group, which consisted of many younger people wearing Trump Wall shirts. Sara Palin also spoke at this rally. This time during the autograph line, I got my little constitution book signed that someone gave me in Appleton, Wisconsin. I said, "I'm back again." Trump said, "I remember you, thank you!"

I headed back to Michigan on April 3, 2016, and it was a very difficult drive home. It was snowing very hard, and the roads were slippery and covered in thick slush, as they had not been plowed. At many times, my top speed was 40 mph.

About a month had passed since my last rally. I watched many rallies online by RSBN, most of which took place in New York. The primary in New York was on April 19, 2016. Donald Trump received eighty-nine delegates, and Kasich came in second place with four delegates.

Around this time, Ted Cruz and John Kasich joined forces to stop Donald Trump. This is what took place: They issued statements saying they would divide their efforts in upcoming contests. Cruz focused on Indiana, and Kasich devoted time to New Mexico and Oregon. The strategy was to block Trump from gaining the 1,237 delegates needed to claim the GOP nomination later that year. Trump called this alliance "pathetic." This is what he thought about it. "If you collude in business, or if you collude in the stock market, they put you in jail. But, in politics, because it's a rigged system, because it's a corrupt enterprise, in politics you're allowed to collude." He added that he had more votes and delegates than Cruz and Kasich combined, although they are long-term politicians.

The Indiana primary took place on May 3, 2016. Donald Trump announced he would do a rally in Fort Wayne, Indiana, on May 1, 2016, at the Allen County War Memorial Coliseum.

### Rally #5 – Ft. Wayne, Indiana 5/1/2016

I arrived at Fort Wayne at 11:00 a.m. I started looking for a hotel; almost all of the hotels were sold out due to some basketball tournaments in the area. As I looked for a room, I pulled into a hotel lot near the Motel 6. I heard a large explosion. Right before that, I saw wires blowing around. I looked in the rearview mirror and saw a huge fireball at the back of my car. I got out of the car and saw people running out of businesses. Someone had hit a telephone pole across the street at a gas station.

I ended up finding a room. Once I did, I stayed in as I had experienced many traffic backups and had seen several accidents.

The morning of the rally, I got in line at 5:00 a.m. There were a couple of people lined up. This venue could hold approximately 15,000 people in total with seats and a floor area.

While waiting for the doors to open at 12:30 p.m., it rained off and on. When we got to the stage area, there was a double barricade. The first area was for VIP. We would have been in the second area—meaning we would not be close enough to get an autograph. Thankfully, I was

7

standing in an area where the barricades unhooked—and the VIP people let some of us in with them. At this rally, Donald Trump told the story of calling Bobby Knight. "I've been waiting for you to call. Is the endorsement still good?" "Absolutely."

This time for my autograph, I had found a Trump coloring book to get signed. He remembered me and asked how we were doing in Indiana. I left the venue at 5:30 p.m. and was home by 11:15 p.m. Another fun trip was in the books. The May 3, 2016, results came in with Trump getting all fifty-seven delegates. Donald Trump had won Indiana.

I had been watching the delegate count very closely, and on May 26, 2016, it was announced that Donald Trump had the 1,237 delegates needed to claim the GOP nomination. I watched a campaign rally online in Bismark, North Dakota. During this speech, he thanked the delegates. He had won the nomination. The final delegate count was 1,441 for Trump and 551 for Cruz.

On May 5, 2016, Donald Trump celebrated Cinco de Mayo at Trump Tower. He published a tweet that read: "Happy #CincoDeMayo! The best taco bowls are made in Trump Grill. I love Hispanics!" That taco bowl looked delicious, and I knew that one day I would travel to Trump Grill and see how they tasted. Since then, I have eaten there several times. Donald Trump was right, it was the best taco bowl I had ever eaten.

On June 24, 2016, Donald Trump was in Scotland for the reopening of his Trump Turnberry Golf Resort. He was there to support his son Eric who represented him in building Turnberry. During this time, the people of the UK had voted to take their country back. Brexit was the withdrawal of the United Kingdom from the European Union.

Donald Trump tweeted: "Just arrived in Scotland. Place is going wild over the vote. They took their county back, just like we will take America back. No games!"

The Republican National Convention was held from July 18 to July 21, 2016. It would take place at the Quicken Loans Arena in Cleveland, Ohio. I had never watched the convention in the past, and I found the speeches very informative. On July 19, Donald Trump, and his running mate, Indiana Governor Mike Pence, were officially nominated as the Republican presidential and vice-presidential candidates.

WikiLeaks leaked emails from top DNC officials that were exchanged from January 2015 through May 2016. Some of the emails showed that these officials tried to find ways to undermine Bernie Sanders' candidacy. Republican nominee Donald Trump said the emails were proof of the Democrats' "rigged" system.

Hillary Clinton drew controversy by using a private server for official public communications. The controversy was a major point of discussion during the 2016 presidential election. The FBI director announced that the FBI investigation had concluded that Clinton had been "extremely careless" but recommended that no charges be filed. It was stated that a Hillary Clinton aide disposed of mobile devices by breaking them with a hammer. Donald Trump's statement: "Crooked H destroyed phones w/hammer, "bleached" emails & had husband meet w/AG days before she was cleared & they talk about obstruction?" – Donald J. Trump (@realDonaldTrump) June 15, 2017.

On August 11, 2016, I watched the Donald Trump rally, which took place in Kissimmee, Florida. It was interesting to see that Donald Trump had some informational cards made up. It was a fast and easy way to explain statistics with graphs and charts.

On August 19, 2016, Louisiana flood victims praised Donald Trump for visiting damaged areas. He stopped at Greenwell Springs Baptist Church on the outskirts of Baton Rouge. He spoke with a small group of flood victims and volunteers, asking a few questions.

## Rally #6 – Dimondale, Michigan 8/9/2016

This rally took place at the Summit Sports and Ice Complex in Dimondale, Michigan, on August 19, 2016. I left on August 18 and drove straight to the venue. Upon arrival, I spoke to the set-up crew so I would know what to expect the next day. I arrived at the venue at 3:30 a.m. There were not many people there yet. So, everyone just sat in their cars. Around 7:00 a.m., a line formed with chairs; it was a very hot day, eighty-five degrees.

They let us in around 2:15 p.m. When I got to the podium area, I saw that there were two barricades. I found the campaign staff I had spoken to the day before and was let into the up-front area. On that day, they selected people to be up there. This rally started late because Donald Trump had visited the Louisiana flood victims earlier in the day, and that made standing harder because of standing in the heat all day.

Someone behind me fainted before the rally started. I was getting very warm and weak, but there was no way for me to get out for water. I held up a twenty-dollar bill and said, "The first person that gets me water can keep the change." Someone jumped on that chance fast, and others behind me thanked me for stating that as they handed the individual money also. Once I had some water I was fine.

Michael Flynn spoke first, and at 5:10 p.m., Donald Trump came out in casual-type clothes and a white MAGA hat as he had just come from the floods. He addressed the crowd, saying, "Thank you, I love Michigan, and come November with your help, we are going to win Michigan, and we are going to win the White House. It's going to be a victory for the people, a victory for the everyday citizen, and for all the people whose voice hasn't been heard. This is going to be your victory."

At the event, there was no rope line (autograph session). The way this venue was set up, it would not allow for that as it was on a dead-end road. There was only one way out, so they needed to get Donald Trump's motorcade out first and then let the people inside the vehicle exit after the motorcade was gone.

In September 2016 at a New York City fundraiser, Hillary Clinton stated that half of Donald Trump's supporters belonged in a "basket of deplorables." This happened just after Hillary Clinton said she would start running a positive campaign. The Trump campaign criticized her comments.

Donald Trump responded to these comments during a speech in Baltimore. This is what he said: "I was deeply shocked and alarmed this Friday to hear my opponent attack, slander, smear, demean these wonderful, amazing people who are supporting our campaign by the millions. Our support comes from every part of America and every walk of life. We have the support of cops and soldiers, carpenters, and welders, the young and the old, and millions of working -class families who just want a better future and a good job. These were the people Hillary Clinton so viciously demonized."

It wasn't long after these comments that shirts popped up all around the country. These are a few that I saw: Deplorables for Trump; Deplorable and Proud; and Proud Member of the Basket of Deplorables.

### Rally #7 – Novi, Michigan 9/30/2016

This rally was at the Suburban Collection Showplace on September 30, 2016. I drove to the venue the day before and checked into The Hyatt, which was attached to the venue. I checked out the venue upon arrival. This was a huge place with many meetings taking place. It was a rainy day, so I stayed in my room on the computer. By 7:00 a.m., people came with chairs to start the line. The doors opened at 2:00 p.m. for the 5:00 p.m. start time.

The stressful part of attending rallies was always, "Will we get to the rope line to get autographs, and will Trump do a rope line?" When I got inside, I was right at the podium, but there were two barricades I noticed to the left; on the side of the stage, there was a single barricade. So, I stood over there to watch the rally from the side, which was also a good spot for viewing his speech.

The rally started out with the usual Michigan Republican speakers. Then General Flynn spoke. After he had finished his speech, he introduced Rudy Giuliani. That was a surprise, as I did not know Rudy was there, and it would be my first time to see him. Then the crowd was excited, awaiting the arrival of Donald Trump to appear on stage. I was on the side where he would walk out; the crowd was enthusiastic and electrifying.

It was amazing to be there and in the front. The crowd continuously chanted, "USA, USA, USA" and "TRUMP, TRUMP, TRUMP!" I had never been to an event like this in my life. My seventh rally was the best one yet. I didn't realize that the line to get in was so long until I saw videos of it online.

Donald Trump's first remarks were, "Thank you everybody, it's so great to be back in Michigan. It's time to rebuild Detroit and be the smart country again."

All the waiting had paid off; his speech was great, and he did the rope line. He started at the far end. The closer he got, the more enthusiastic the crowd became. This time, I had my small two-inch book held way out to sign, got that done, and shook his hand. He said, "Are we going to win Michigan?" I said, "It's close. Come back at the end of October." And guess what, he came back on October 31, 2016.

On September 12, 2016, Trump International Hotel in Washington, DC, opened. He held an event there on September 16 for Medal of Honor winners. I remember watching this on television. He spoke about the hotel, stating it was under budget and ahead of schedule. It was one of the greatest hotels in the world, and I can agree to that, as I have stayed there and eaten there several times. Later in the day, I saw this statement: "Donald Trump fooled cable news into a 25-minute infomercial for his campaign."

On September 23, 2016, Ted Cruz endorsed Donald Trump for president of the United States.

"After many months of careful consideration of prayer and searching my own conscience, I have decided that on Election Day I will vote for the Republican nominee, Donald Trump," Cruz wrote in a Facebook post.

Donald Trump responded, saying, "I am greatly honored by the endorsement of Senator Cruz. We have fought the battle and he was a tough and brilliant opponent. I look forward to working with him for many years to come in order to Make America Great Again."

I remember hearing these words while I watched his speech on television from West Palm Beach, Florida, on October 13, 2016.

"There is nothing the political establishment will not do. No lie they won't tell, to hold their prestige and power at your expense, and that's what's been happening. The Washington establishment and the financial and media corporations that fund it, exist for only one reason, to protect and enrich itself."

On October 14, 2016, Donald Trump held a campaign rally in Charlotte, North Carolina, at the PNC Music Pavilion. I watched this on television. All of a sudden, he said, "These teleprompters haven't been working for the last twenty minutes, and I actually like my speech better without teleprompters. You know what? I like it better without the teleprompter. Get this thing outta here, will you?" He continued his speech without the teleprompters, as he doesn't need them anyway.

As Election Day grew closer, things started to heat up. A Republican Party headquarters in North Carolina was firebombed, and a nearby building was vandalized. The building was a total loss, and thankfully no one was injured.

## Rally # 8 – Grand Rapids, Michigan 10/31/2016

We spent Halloween morning with Donald Trump in Grand Rapids, Michigan, at the DeltaPlex Arena. On October 30, I drove to Grand Rapids and checked out the venue. I was familiar with this one because I was there in December 2015 for my first Trump rally. After this, I had lunch at Fazoli's and checked into the Holiday Inn. I spent the day in the hotel watching the rallies that took place in Las Vegas.

I left for the venue at 3:00 a.m. Not many people were there yet. The regular early rally goers were on the other side of the state waiting in line for the Warren, Michigan, rally. The stage was set up nice with a fall scene, which consisted of mums, pumpkins, and hay bales.

At this one, I noticed once again the double barricades. But at the left of the stage there was a single one, so I stood over there in order to see better. Michael Flynn and Bobby Knight spoke at this one, which was filled to capacity. They did not have time to do the rope line, as they needed to get to the second rally of the day in Warren, Michigan.

The drive home went by fast as there was very little traffic, and I was entertained by listening to the Warren, Michigan, rally, which was on the radio.

## Rally #9 – Sterling Heights, Michigan 11/6/2016

My ninth rally was held on November 6, 2016, in Sterling Heights, Michigan, at the Freedom Hill Amphitheater. I left home at 10:30 a.m., drove all night to then sleep in the car. This was confusing for entry, as they didn't want anyone in the lot until later, and they didn't have a time set for people to come in. Everyone just drove up and down the major road waiting to see cars being allowed in. By the time I got in line, there were at least ten in line. I saw people I knew at this one.

It was a sunny day, and this was a nice outdoor amphi-theater with chairs. When I got inside, I noticed that at least the first ten rows were for VIP. After sitting there awhile, all of a sudden, everyone moved up a couple of rows by climbing over the chairs. I wasn't expecting to move, and at that time, I ended up cracking my phone screen, and the zoom lens of my camera did not function properly due to it falling on the cement. These two items needed to be replaced anyway, so that was done after I arrived home.

On this particular day, there were two rallies ahead of ours; Sioux City, Iowa, and Minneapolis, Minnesota. Our rally was to start at 6:00 p.m., but it was ninety minutes late. We were entertained by Ted Nugent as we waited. This was the most enthusiastic crowd to date. Trump did not sign autographs at this one because he had two more speeches to make at Moon Township, Pennsylvania, and Leesburg, Virginia.

When I got to the lot, the motorcade had just pulled away. When I turned on the radio to Fox News in the car, they mentioned that a large crowd was waiting for Trump to speak in Moon Township, Pennsylvania. That rally had an 8:00 p.m. start time; ours did not start until about 7:30 p.m. The last two rallies of the five scheduled for the day had a much later start time. But the supporters didn't mind because it was always worth the wait. The time driving home all night went by fast because once the next rally started, I was able to listen to it on the radio on Fox News.

Donald Trump's last campaign rally was held in Grand Rapids, Michigan, at the Devos Convention Center at 11:00 p.m. on November 7, 2016. This would be his fifth stop of the day, and the rally started after midnight, so technically, he did his final speech of the campaign on Election Day. I listened to it online.

I remember the speech went something like this, "Hello, Michigan! I'm Mike Pence. I'm the Governor of Indiana. It's one minute after midnight, the day we are going to Make America Great Again." Donald Trump took the stage next and said, "It's now officially Tuesday, November 8. Did you ever think you would hear a major speech at around one o'clock in the morning?" Toward the end of the speech, he said, "The election is now, it's today, hours away from the change you've been waiting for."

It was finally November 8, 2016, Election Day, the day many of us had waited for. Which candidate would get at least 270 electors to win the presidential election?

I watched the election results from home. I checked out all the stations to see what they had to say. As time went on, I remember a particular journalist kept looking at the map and trying to find a path of victory for Hillary Clinton. At one point, I remember him saying, "we" can still win.

Watching this election was a very exciting and nerve-wracking time. When I think back on this now, I remember thinking, "How can we beat this Clinton establishment machine?"

The Trump campaign watch party was at the New York Hilton Midtown, which was not open to the public. The Clinton campaign had a watch party that was open to the public at the Jacob K. Javitz Convention Center. Hillary Clinton's campaign chair, John Podesta, took the stage at the Democratic election night watch party in New York City alone and delivered a simple message: "Everybody should go home." Hillary Clinton did not make an appearance at the Javitz Center.

Donald Trump said he received a call from Clinton shortly before he gave a victory speech early Wednesday in Manhattan. He was declared President-elect at 2:30 a.m. with 306 electoral votes to Clinton's 227.

Donald Trump gave his victory speech early Wednesday morning. He said, "I pledge to every citizen of our land that I will be president for all Americans, and this is so important to me. For those who have chosen not to support me in the past, of which there were a few people, I'm reaching out to you for your guidance and your help so that we can work together and unify our great country."

What a relief, the election was over, and Donald Trump won! The headlines of the local paper here said, "Trump Shocks Political World." Donald Trump's victory, with no government experience, was a powerful rejection of the establishment forces that assembled against him.

The Trump team planned to do a Thank-You Tour after Thanksgiving. He held a rally in states that supported him and swing states that supported a Republican for president for the first time in decades. The states he visited on the Thank-You Tour were as follows: Cincinnati, Ohio; Fayetteville, North Carolina; Des Moines, Iowa; Baton Rouge, Louisiana; Grand Rapids, Michigan; Hershey, Pennsylvania; Orlando, Florida; and Mobile, Alabama.

## Rally #10 – Grand Rapids, Michigan 12/9/2016

I was thankful that one of the Thank-You Tour rallies was in my home state. I arrived at 3:00 a.m. on December 9, 2016. They allowed people to stay in their cars until 8:00 a.m., then the gate was closed for entry until 11:00 a.m. I had been to the DeltaPlex for my first rally, so this venue was familiar to me.

After 11:00 a.m., the line of chairs formed. It was cold outside with light snowfall. I was able to get right in the front, not far from the podium. He started the rally by saying, "I'm here tonight for one main reason, to say thank you to the incredible people of Michigan."

This was another full house with standing room only and a large overflow crowd outside. I had completed ten rallies on the campaign trail, and I enjoyed every moment. I heard so much and made some incredible friends along the way.

# Chapter 2

# January 2017 to June 2017

———— ★ ————

The inauguration of President Donald J. Trump took place on Friday, January 20, 2017. I had never been to Washington, DC, so I decided to go.

**My Journey to Washington, DC**

On Tuesday, January 17, I drove to the airport to catch my flight. The plane left a bit late, as it needed to be de-iced. My next flight was from Detroit to Washington Dulles. I arrived just before noon. The airport was about twenty-five miles from downtown. I took a shuttle for twenty-nine dollars and was dropped off at my hotel, Club Quarters.

The hotel was nice with a small lobby and a restaurant right off of it. The hotel had 160 rooms. On the second floor, there was a lounge area with two computers and a printer. The fridge was stocked with pop, and they also had free snacks.

It was a rainy day. I first walked over to Trump International Hotel. It was so nice. I went into the lobby and looked around. The lobby area was beautiful with chandeliers and a lounge area. After viewing Trump International, I walked around the White House area. I got back to Club Quarters at 6:30 p.m. The special at the restaurant was nachos, so I had those to go, which were delicious.

I headed out early Wednesday morning. I decided to walk down toward the White House, which was four blocks away. While I was there, I ended up speaking with a student from Australia. It was so interesting to hear his story. He had been following the Trump campaign since the primaries and knew he had to be here. So, $2,000.00 and eighteen hours later, he made it.

I then walked over to the Lincoln Memorial area, which was the site for the Make America Great welcome celebration. They set up the stage for this event. I ended up receiving four tickets to the inauguration. The two red tickets were about halfway back, and the two silver tickets were further back.

I was glad that I went to Trump International on the first day I arrived. The second day I was there, it was all blocked off, and you could only go in if you were staying there. This was due to the night before, at 7:00 p.m., a man set himself on fire in the middle of the road in front of Trump Hotel.

Later that evening, I was near Trump International Hotel, taking pictures. I received a message that Donald Trump had landed in DC and was going to dinner with Mike Pence. A couple of minutes later, I saw the motorcade approach. It was super exciting to record it, and it sure was noisy with sirens, a helicopter, many motorcycles at the front, and a lot of black Chevrolet Suburbans.

I ended up seeing the motorcade three times that night. The helicopter would start circling in a small area, then one knew the motorcade would be seen shortly.

On Thursday, January 19, I headed to the Lincoln Memorial for the MAGA Welcome Celebration. The gate opened at 10:30 a.m., and it was like walking through a park to get there. I was on the left side of the reflecting pool, and not far from there, they had performances throughout the day. The main performers were from 4:00 p.m. to 6:00 p.m. Toby Keith was the last to perform. Then Lee Greenwood sang "God Bless the USA." Donald Trump was the last one to speak. After he finished, there was a very nice display of fireworks.

## January 20, 2017

Finally, it was the day we were waiting for. I got on the metro at 5:00 a.m. and got in the red gate line; a lot of people were there already.

It was thirty-five degrees and still dark when they let us in the gate at 6:15 a.m. After the gate opened, everyone ran to get in line for the security check. As soon as I got through security, it was another run to find the best place to stand in the red ticket section.

Music played, and they played the history of the White House on the big screen. Donald Trump was sworn in right at noon. Here are a couple of highlights from his speech:

Today's ceremony, however, has a very special meaning because today we are not merely transferring power from one administration to another, or from one party to another, but we are transferring power from Washington, DC,

23

and giving it back to you, the people. What truly matters is not which party controls our government but whether our government is controlled by the people. January 20, 2017, will be remembered as the day the people became the rulers of this nation again. The forgotten men and women of our country will be forgotten no longer.

After Donald Trump's speech, I took my time walking over to the parade route. I had a VIP ticket for the parade, which stated I had a seat on the bleachers near the Department of Treasury building. The parade lasted from 3:30 to 6:30 p.m.

On Saturday, June 21, 2017, I flew out of Washington, DC, to Detroit. Upon arrival to Detroit, my flight was delayed and then canceled. I slept on the floor of the airport. On Sunday, all of the flights home were canceled again. There were four other people headed in my direction that were also stranded. We split a rental car, and I was home Sunday night, and my suitcase made it home a few days later.

The trip to Washington, DC, was one of the best trips of my lifetime. I am so thankful I was able to attend the inauguration and meet so many great people.

On January 20, 2017, Donald Trump signed his first executive order, which directed the federal government to begin dismantling Obamacare.

On February 18, 2017, Donald Trump held his first rally as president of the United States. The rally was in Melbourne, Florida, at the Orlando Melbourne Airport.

Melania Trump spoke first. "Good afternoon. It is my honor and great pleasure to stand here before you as the first lady of the United States. I will act in the best interest of all of you." She then introduced President Donald Trump:

It is so great to be here in Florida, my second home. This is a state I truly love. This is a state where we all had a great victory together; thank you. It's now been a month since my inauguration, and I am here to tell you about our incredible progress in Making

American Great Again. I'm also here to tell you about our plans for the future, and they're big, and they're bold, and it's what our country is all about.

## Rally #11 – Louisville, Kentucky 3/20/2017

It was announced that Donald Trump would hold a rally on March 20, 2017 in Louisville, Kentucky at the Kentucky Exposition Center. I decided to go. The trip was planned at the last minute and would be my first rally with Donald Trump as president. I arrived at this rally by car around 9:30 a.m., and took my place in line. Upon entering the venue, I saw that the floor area was filled with chairs. I sat in the second row.

The anticipation of Donald Trump walking out on stage never gets old. The closer it got to showtime, the more enthusiastic the crowd became. I had never experienced anything like it.

President Donald Trump walked to the podium and said, "Thank you, thank you, everybody. I am thrilled to be here in the great state of Kentucky and the beautiful city of Louisville, and this place is packed." The venue was packed from the floor to the ceiling with so much enthusiasm for the president of the United States.

He closed with this: "So with hope in our souls, and patriotism in our hearts, let us now recite these words. Are you ready? Together, we will make America strong again. We will make America wealthy again. We will make America proud again. We will make America safe again. And we will Make American Great Again."

After the rally, I had dinner at a close-by restaurant, stayed at the Holiday Inn, and was home the next day.

On February 25, 2017, it was announced that Trump would be the first president in thirty-six years to skip the White House correspondents' dinner. His tweet read like this: "I will not be attending the White House Correspondents Association dinner this year. Please wish everyone well and have a great evening!"

It was announced that Donald Trump would be heading to Harrisburg, Pennsylvania, to celebrate his first hundred days in office. This rally was timed to coincide with the annual dinner of the White House press corps in Washington, which he declined to attend.

## Rally #12 – Harrisburg, Pennsylvania 4/29/2017

This rally would mark Donald Trump's one hundredth day in office. It was held at the Farm Show Complex & Expo Center. I arrived at the venue by car. A long line had already formed. I took my place in line and enjoyed my day visiting in line. I entered this venue from the top area and then had to maze through the seats to find a good standing spot near the podium. Vice President Mike Pence spoke at this rally, and it was my first time to see him.

Next came President Donald Trump. As usual, the crowd went wild with cheers. This is what he said toward the beginning of his speech:

As you know, there's another big gathering taking place tonight in Washington, DC. Did you hear about it? A large group of Hollywood actors and Washington media are consoling each other in a hotel ballroom in our nation's capital right now.

They are gathered together for the White House Correspondents' Dinner without the president. And I could not possibly be more thrilled than to be more than one hundred miles away from Washington's swamp, spending my evening with all of you, and with a much, much larger crowd and much better people, right?

The rallies became larger, and the lines to get in became longer. After the one hundredth day rally, I drove the 810 miles straight to home.

### Rally #13 – Cedar Rapids, Iowa 6/21/2017

This rally was held at US Cellular Center on June 21, 2017. I arrived at this rally at around 7:00 a.m. By the time I arrived, there were about ten people there, so I pulled out my chair and placed it in line to wait for the doors to open. This was actually a very nice setup, as there was a Double Tree by Hilton hotel attached to the venue. I made a reservation there so I would have a place to stay after the rally.

When the doors to the venue opened, I was able to get a spot close to the podium again. President Donald Trump came out and thanked the crowd for being there. He stated that it was always great to leave the Washington swamp and spend time with the working people. I remember a protester started blowing a whistle in an attempt to disrupt the rally. "Never fails," Donald Trump remarked. The crowd started cheering, "USA, USA, USA!"

After the rally, I headed to my room, which was steps away. The next day, I took in some of the sights and drove home.

# Chapter 3

# March 2018 to December 2018

### Rally #14 – Moon Township, Pennsylvania 3/10/2018

I t had been quite a while since I had attended a Trump rally, as there were not many scheduled during that time.

The Trump campaign announced that they would hold a campaign rally in Moon Township, Pennsylvania, on March 10, 2018. The rally was scheduled to start at 7:00 p.m. at Atlantic Aviation. The president was looking forward to visiting the Pittsburgh area to highlight the benefits his historic tax cuts were providing hardworking families across Pennsylvania and celebrate our booming economy now that America was once again open for business.

Also, this rally would happen three days before the 18th Congressional District special election, pitting Republican State Representative Rick Saccone against Democrat Conor Lamb.

As I traveled to this rally, there was breaking news. President Trump agreed to meet Kim Jong Un. President Trump agreed to meet with Kim Jong Un after Kim pledged to refrain from further nuclear tests and move toward denuclearization. It was an invitation by the leader of North Korea to meet face to face with the president of the United States.

As I got closer to the venue, I found it confusing to find the exact spot that this rally would take place. On my phone, I saw someone doing a live Facebook video describing the whereabouts of the rally. I called her and found out where to go. I had arrived twenty-six hours before the start of the rally.

There was a Sheetz within walking distance. I had never been to one before and found that this was a great place to get food. It was a very cold night, and many people were spending the night in their cars. I spent the night in a tent with a girl I had met that day. When I woke up in the morning, my contact lens case had popped open, as the liquid inside was partially frozen. The sun was coming out, and we had a pleasant time waiting for the doors to open. The line got very long, and many people had made signs regarding Nancy Pelosi's "crumbs" statement. One of the signs said, "Donald, thank you for the crumbs." Some corporations gave out bonuses to their employees, which Nancy called crumbs. The president stated that bonuses of a few thousand dollars were not crumbs, it was a lot of money.

Another successful rally was in the books. I found a nice spot to stand up near the podium and made some more friends.

When this rally ended, it was a race to get to the PPG Paints Arena in Pittsburgh. The tickets were still available online. So, after the car was parked, a ticket was purchased, and I entered the venue just as Kid Rock had started to perform. After the concert, it was off to the Double Tree for the night to rest before making the journey home.

On March 13, 2018, President Trump visited California to see prototypes near the Mexico border. President Trump examined eight recently constructed prototypes for the wall near the US–Mexico border in San Diego to pick the right one. He mentioned that a border wall was truly the first line of defense.

President Trump signed an executive order in January 2017, ordering the immediate construction of a border wall, though more specifics came a year later in a request his Department of Homeland Security made to Congress for the needed cash.

On April 6, 2018, it was announced that President Trump would once again skip the White House Correspondents' dinner. This boycott began during his first year in office.

This was good news for rally goers, as they knew there would be a rally that would coincide with the correspondents' dinner once again. Where would it be this time? I was hoping for Michigan.

On April 17, 2018, the Trump Campaign announced a campaign rally in Washington Township, Michigan, at the Total Sports Park. The rally would be held on April 28, 2018.

## Rally #15 – Washington Township, Michigan 4/28/2018

I arrived at this rally the day before, so I could check out the venue and visit the surrounding area. Being that this was my fifteenth rally, I was starting to meet up with some of the regulars. It was nice to have people to visit with while waiting for the event to start. At this particular venue, people stayed overnight in their cars on a side road waiting for the go-ahead to park on the grassy field to then line up.

When the gates to the field opened, everyone drove in on an uneven field to then get out of the vehicle, grab chairs, and run to the area where the line of chairs would start. After your sport was secured with your chair, you could go back and forth to your vehicle as needed. Usually, about an hour before the doors opened to these events, people would secure their belongings in their vehicles. The less that was brought through security, the better.

Upon entering the venue, I was able to find a spot to stand right near the podium. And as always, the room was full of energy awaiting the president of the United States— Donald J. Trump. I liked this part of the speech: "You may have heard, I was invited to another correspondents' dinner, but I'd much rather be in Washington, Michigan than Washington, DC; that I can tell you."

There was not a close airport for President Trump to land, so he was in a motorcade with some Michigan congressmen. It was at this time he first heard about the need to rebuild the Soo Locks.

The next day, on April 28, 2018, the Detroit News stated that President Donald Trump's unexpected embrace of a half-billion dollar Soo Locks modernization project had given new momentum to a three-decade effort to update the aging freight passage infrastructure in Michigan's upper peninsula.

On May 8, 2018, I was a passenger in a vehicle headed to the Newark, New Jersey, airport. I was less than ten miles from the airport when I noticed a Trump rally was scheduled for Elkhart, Indiana, on May 10. I was to land back in the United States on May 8, so I could make this work. There wasn't much time to make arrangements, but I was able to extend my trip for a couple more days to fit this event in.

It was off to Trump International Doonbeg and Cork, Ireland, to see an Ed Sheeran concert. I flew back to Newark,

New Jersey on the evening of May 8. It was time to start the drive to Elkhart, Indiana. I slept at a rest area for a while and made it to Elkhart the next day.

## Rally #16 – Elkhart, Indiana 5/10/2018

This rally was held at Northside Middle School on May 10, 2018. I arrived at the property late in the afternoon. I spent the day visiting with others in line, then chose to sleep in a sleeping bag for the night outside.

The next day, the line was long, all through the close-by neighborhood streets. By the time the venue opened, the back of the line was up by the front of the line. But, when the doors opened, I was able to get a good spot to stand near the podium area. After the rally, I drove straight home since I had been away for so long.

On May 18, 2018, it was announced that President Trump would hold a rally at the Municipal Auditorium during his May 29th visit to Nashville for a fundraiser for Republican Senate Candidate Marsha Blackburn.

## Rally #17 – Nashville, Tennessee 5/29/2018

I already had plans to be in New York City for Memorial Day weekend to do some sightseeing and eat at Trump Grill. So, I drove to Nashville by way of New York City. I arrived at the Nashville Municipal Auditorium at 5:00 a.m. the morning of the rally. A line of chairs had already formed, so I joined the line and waited for the doors to open. The line had moved a couple of times, which caused some disruptions. But when the doors opened, it was easy to get to the front area near the podium once again.

Instead of driving all the way home after the rally, I stayed at a beautiful bed and breakfast in Brush Creek, Tennessee. The next day, it was a beautiful drive home through Tennessee and Kentucky. I didn't want the trip to end.

On May 30, 2018, Kim Kardashian met with President Trump at the White House. She talked about the president possibly granting clemency to Alice Marie Johnson, a sixty-three-year-old nonviolent drug offender currently serving a life sentence behind bars. Later, President Trump tweeted this: "Great meeting with @KimKardashian today, talked about prison reform and sentencing." – 6:59 p.m. May 30, 2018

After Kim Kardashian personally advocated for her at the White House, President Trump commuted the sentence of Alice Marie Johnson. On June 14, 2018, Kardashian and Johnson sat down for their first in-person meeting.

On June 6, 2018, it was announced that the much-anticipated meeting between US President Donald Trump and

North Korean leader Kim Jong Un would take place at a hotel on the Singaporean island of Sentosa.

The US had stressed that it wanted to see steps toward complete, verifiable, and irreversible denuclearization of North Korea before sanctions relief could be implemented.

The summit began with a striking image that was unimaginable months before. The two men walked toward each other and firmly gripped each other's hands in front of US and North Korean flags.

"It was not easy to get here," Mr. Kim said. "There were obstacles, but we overcame them to be here."

The two men, accompanied only by interpreters, spoke for a little under forty minutes. They were then joined by small delegations of advisors for a working lunch.

## Rally #18 – Duluth, Minnesota 6/20/2018

I left for this rally on June 19, and I arrived at the Amsoil Arena the following morning. The line-up for this rally weaved through a very warm parking garage. A couple of people fainted before getting inside. After the doors to the venue opened, it was time to maze through the seated area to then find a place to the podium area. The rally had extremely high energy with a lot of first-time goers.

The venue was not far from many restaurants. I decided to eat the Grandma's Saloon. Then I walked along the water and across the aerial lock bridge. I stayed at the Radisson Hotel for the night. The next day, I made the drive home.

I approached the Flint area and noticed someone following me. They passed me, slowed right down in front of me, then got behind me. I called 911, as I thought they would try to run me off the road. It was 3:30 a.m., and I was kept on the line and told what to do. They had me exit at the next police-type exit when I left I-75 to take the exit. The car that was following me kept going. I met up with the police at a gas station. They talked to me for a while and said they were having problems with gangs running cars off the road. I was relieved to finally make it home after that incident.

### Rally #19 – Fargo, North Dakota 6/27/2018

My nineteenth rally took place at Scheels Arena in Fargo, North Dakota. This was a long drive, and I ended up in the car all night to get to the venue a few hours before the doors opened. Luckily, I was still able to get a standing spot right up front. This venue had a capacity of 6,000, and it was estimated that 15,000 could not get in.

After the rally, I drove to the Detroit area because I would be attending a concert at DTE before heading home.

At a rally in Great Falls, Montana, on July 5, 2018, President Trump challenged Democratic Senator Elizabeth Warren to prove her Native American heritage. "I will give you $1 million to your favorite charity if you take the test and it shows you are an Indian, and let's see what she does. I have a feeling she will say no."

On July 6, 2018, it was stated that when Mike Pompeo met Kim Jung-un in Pyongyang, he would reportedly attempt to smooth a path toward denuclearization with a gift that playfully references a low point in relations between the North Korean leader and President Trump; a CD of Elton John's Rocket Man. Several times the year before, Trump referred to the dictator as "Little Rocket Man."

On August 10, 2018, the Trump campaign announced that the next "Make America Great Again" rally would be held in Charleston, West Virginia, on August 21. President

Trump would urge residents to vote for the Republican candidates in the midterm elections, including West Virginia Attorney General Patrick Morrisey, who was running for US Senate against Democratic Senator Joe Manchin. He would also speak on the economy, national security, and Supreme Court nominee Brett Kavanaugh.

## Rally #20 – Charleston, West Virginia 8/21/2018

This rally took place at the Civic Center. When I arrived at the venue, the line was actually inside a mall. This was nice; you could leave your chair, head to the food court, and bring some food back to eat before the doors to the venue opened. Upon entering this arena, I was at the top area and had to quickly do the maze through the seats, then find a way to the floor. I did this very quickly and got right to the podium area. I was the only one down there. I did not know what had happened. Eventually, everyone made it to the floor. The staff had stopped people and wanted to first fill some of the seated sections. That didn't sit well with people that had been waiting for hours to get a close viewing spot for the rally.

During the rally, President Trump said he'd be hitting the road frequently leading up to the November midterm elections. "We're going to be out a lot, as much as I'm allowed to, but sometimes the Secret Service holds you back. Maybe I'll do a couple trips without them."

President Trump also mentioned that he gave Ron DeSantis a nice tweet, and he went from three to twenty.

After the rally, it was time to have a post rally meal with friends and head to the Holiday Inn for the night.

## Rally #21 – Evansville, Indiana 8/30/2018

An article came out before the rally stating that Ford Center expected thousands to attend the August 30 rally. The capacity of the venue is 11,000. I arrived at the venue at 7:00 p.m. and set up my sleeping bag in front of the Ford Center. Several people were already in line. At 9:00 a.m., we needed to move the line to the sidewalk, so we made a line of chairs over there. This was another venue that when you entered, you were at the top and had to maze down and find a way to the floor area. I had found a good viewing spot right in front of the podium.

During the speech, President Trump said that people came up to him all the time and would say, "Thank you for saving our country." The country was choking with regulations.

> Instead of apologizing for America, we are standing tall for America, the country that we love. We are

standing up for the heroes who protect America. We are proudly standing up for our national anthem.

We will never give up. We will never give in. We will never back down. And we will fight on to victory. We will only have victory because we are Americans and our hearts bleed red, white, and blue.

After the rally, I walked to a really unique restaurant. It used to be a Greyhound Station, and then it was off to the nearby DoubleTree to get some rest before the drive home the following day.

### Rally #22 – Las Vegas, Nevada 9/20/2018

I was excited to learn that there would be a rally in Las Vegas, as there was so much to see and do there. I headed out at 2:00 p.m. on September 18, and traveled across the International Bridge to Canada. I arrived at the Sault Ste. Marie, Ontario Airport, at 2:30 p.m. My forty-seven-minute flight to Toronto left at 4:40 p.m. I ate dinner at the Toronto airport, then it was time to board the plane for Las Vegas. I arrived at 10:30 p.m. and took a Lyft to the back of Harrah's and cut through the Flamingo. I then walked over to the food court across from Excalibur, but they were about to close.

I decided to walk to the Taco Bell; it was very nice with booths right at the front to sit and view the strip. I had a taco and some lemonade and charged by phone. I sat here at my usual booth until 5:00 a.m.

I decided to walk the strip and check out the convention center. It was still dark out, and not a lot of people around. There were staff cleaning the sidewalks of the fronts of the casinos by spraying them with a hose. I turned right on Convention Center Drive to then walk to the venue. I was told that the rally would be at North Hall. I was just killing time to use the free pool at the Flamingo.

When I arrived at the Flamingo at 8:15 a.m., a line had already started to form. The gate for the Go Pool opened at 9:00 a.m. I found a lounge chair to relax in, as I had been up all night. I got talking to the people in the chairs next to me, and they were also going to the rally. Later on, I decided to walk around and purchase a couple of souvenirs, all while pulling my small suitcase.

Before heading back to the Convention Center, I stopped for something to eat at the Fashion Show Mall food court. They have delicious spaghetti, pizza, and salads. When I arrived at the Convention Center lobby, I could see the whole setup. At that time, they were testing the equipment and music.

At 10:00 p.m., the line started forming on the cement just down from the entrance. It was a relaxing night to sleep on the ground, as it had cooled off. Eventually, at the rallies, someone shows up that you know, so I was able to store my suitcase in a vehicle.

After being in the hot sun in line all day, I noticed that my watch looked odd. It had fried from the heat and was no longer working.

It was a nice place to wait in line, as you could go in and out of the Convention Center to cool off. After the gates opened, I just walked right into the large room and was able to get to the front near the podium. As soon as the rally ended, I got a Lyft to the airport, as my flight left at 11:20 p.m. I had a stop in Montreal, then it was on to Toronto. The plane sat on the runway in Toronto for quite a while, as they were trying to fix the air conditioning. Once the plane finally took off, they announced that we might not be able to land at the Soo, Ontario airport because of a storm and high winds and would have to land at the Pellston Airport seventy-five miles away to wait the storm out.

As it turned out, we landed in Soo Ontario. Since this was a very small plane, when it landed, you would walk down the stairs and outside to the airport. The winds were very strong; it was hard to stand up. But, it was a short walk to the car. Another successful rally was in the books.

## Rally #23 – Johnson City, Tennessee 10/1/2018

The Johnson City rally was held at Freedom Hall, which was on a school property. I arrived in Johnson City at 2:00 p.m. the day before the rally. Setting up the line for entry to this rally was very confusing, as the line was moved many times.

At 5:00 p.m., the first attempt was made. Not long after that, the cars needed to be moved from the lot; since we were in the neighborhood, we got permission to put five cars in a neighbor's driveway. Later in the evening, the line changed again. It wasn't very close to where the cars were parked, but we decided to leave the cars in that driveway, as they were safe there until the conclusion of the rally the next day.

By 2:00 a.m., we were told that another line had formed across from the venue. By this time, all the people that arrived first were behind the people that started this line in the middle of the night. We were able to get a little sleep by lying on the ground in sleeping bags. At 7:00 a.m., we walked about a mile to the car to change clothes and drop off unneeded items.

At 9:00 a.m., they let us walk across the street to then wait for the doors to open. The line of people waiting to get in was so long you could not see the end of it. I had forgotten to take my watch off, and being that the car was so far away I buried it in the ground right near the line going in. I like to have as little with me, so you have a quick time going through security. Although there were many going into the venue ahead of me, I was able to get up front by the podium. When I got outside, it was dark, and I was having a hard time finding my watch that I had buried. A man saw me looking for it and said he saw me put it right around a certain area. Sure enough, there it was. I also retrieved my chair. I had a post-rally meal and was home the next day.

On October 6, 2018, the divisive fight in the senate over President Trump's Supreme Court nominee, Judge Brett M. Kavanaugh, reached an end with a vote of fifty to forty-eight to elevate the judge to the nation's highest court.

The confirmation had dominated headlines for weeks, inspiring protests and encouraging women to share personal stories. Lindsey Graham was all over the news. The quote I remember most was, "If you're looking for a fair process, you came to the wrong town." Later that day, Brett Kavanaugh was sworn in as Supreme Court Justice.

## Rally #24 – Lebanon, Ohio 10/12/2018

It was announced that President Donald Trump would visit Lebanon, Ohio, as he toured battleground areas to motivate supporters to turn out for Republican candidates in the upcoming mid-term elections.

I arrived at the Warren County fairgrounds at 10:30 p.m. the night before the rally. We started the line around the main road going in. We stayed at a hotel across the street for a little while. The line was long and very orderly. The fairgrounds were surrounded by big fences, so this would have been a great setup, except for the fact that there was another gate all the way down near the 500th person in line.

As it got closer to the 2:00 p.m. mark, the cars on the busy road drove back and forth and went very slowly at the entrance, as they wanted to be there when the gate opened. This also caused extreme traffic problems as people would sit at the gate in moving traffic. The people in line would be let in first, then the cars would follow.

At 2:00 p.m., both gates opened, and it was a very long run on uneven terrain, to then stand in line to wait to go through security. I had never seen anything like it. It was like a stampede; people lost their shoes and fell to the ground. When I got to the security area, I noticed there were about ten magnetometers, and everyone had formed lines in the first three. I saw many empty ones down to the right and ended up in line over there.

We only had to wait here about thirty minutes. Then it was a short distance to be in the front area. Some of the people up front became very angry because there were two barricades, and they were randomly putting people up front, so now they could not see. They were upset because they waited all day, and random people that just got there were in front. They stated, "We donate to the campaign every month, and this is the thanks we get." I apologized to them, saying, "President Trump does not know this is going on," and "Please still vote for him." They agreed on that, thankfully.

After the rally, it started to rain hard, and it was a muddy walk out of there, so I didn't go back to get my chair.

On Thursday, October 18, it was announced that the rally was moved from the NRG Arena to the Toyota Center in response to tickets. I did not attend the MAGA rally in Houston, Texas, on October 22, 2018. I had decided to go to a couple of Donald Trump Jr. rallies. The first one was in Pontiac, Michigan, on October 17. It was to support John James for US senator. Ted Nugent and Kid Rock performed.

The second rally was in Greenfield, Indiana, on October 22 to support Mike Braun for Senate. These two rallies were on a smaller scale, so after the rallies, Donald Trump Jr. signed autographs.

The US president's aircraft was spotted by an aviation enthusiast as it flew over the United Kingdom on its second visit to the US troops in Iraq.

On Wednesday, December 26, President Donald Trump and First Lady Melania Trump greeted the military at the dining hall during an unannounced visit to Al Asad Airbase in Iraq.

# Chapter 4

# March 2019 to December 2019

———— ★ ————

In March 2019, the Mueller Report concluded that its investigation did not find sufficient evidence that the campaign coordinated or conspired with the Russian government in election interference activities.

### Rally #25 – Grand Rapids, Michigan 3/28/2019

I arrived at the Van Andel Arena just before noon. I parked on the bridge near Grand Valley State and walked around downtown for a while. I decided to have lunch at the Big Boy since the line had yet to form. Once my friend arrived, we decided to find a place to put our cars. We ended up using Ellis Parking Lot, which was great. It was a lot that held approximately sixty vehicles and was at a great location.

We decided to start the line at 7:00 p.m. with our sleeping bags. A little bit later, others started to line up as well. It was a cold night, but partway through the night, I felt quite warm. That is when I noticed we were sleeping on heated sidewalks.

I walked over to Lucky Luciano's for a delicious piece of pizza before entering the rally. Upon entering, it was easy to get a spot up front since I was familiar with the arena from attending concerts here in the past.

Donald Trump Jr. came on stage and threw MAGA hats into the crowd. The crowd started chanting, "USA, USA, USA!" He said, "Imagine if you chanted that at a Democrat rally." President Trump came out on stage and said, "This has been a couple of incredible weeks for America. The Russian hoax is finally dead. I could have told you that two and a half years ago. Think of the time wasted. They refused to accept the results of the 2016 election."

On April 15, 2019, President Trump said that he would skip the White House Correspondents dinner again and hold a rally instead. "The dinner is boring and so negative that we're going to hold a very positive rally. I will be in Green Bay, Wisconsin, on Saturday, April 27 at the Resch Center – Big crown expected! #MAGA."

## Rally #26 – Green Bay, Wisconsin 4/27/2019

I arrived at the Resch Center at 3:00 p.m. There were a few people there just sitting around on benches. There was a restaurant and Best Western next door. I was able to pay twenty dollars to park my car there.

Some people from California stopped by the line in the evening. They brought pizza, pop, and coffee for the people staying out all night. It got down to thirty-five degrees, but it wasn't bad since I was in a tent. The time waiting in line always went quickly when it was rally day. It was an easy entry to find a close spot by the podium. I had a post rally meal at Fazoli's and drove home the next day.

On May 13, 2019, it was announced that President Trump would tour Montoursville, Pennsylvania, with State Representative Fred Keller the day before the primary and special elections next week.

## Rally #27 – Montoursville, Pennsylvania 5/20/2019

I arrived at the Energy Aviation hangar at 10:00 p.m. the night before the rally. After speaking to the staff inside the office, I decided to get a close-by hotel since it was raining and the road to get close to the venue was blocked off.

At 6:00 a.m., I headed back, and there were only about ten people in line. By 7:30 a.m., a staff led the line closer to the hangar area. They had a lot of food trucks, so I had lunch before entering the hangar. It was a very short distance to find a viewing spot. I chose to be in the front by the podium.

It was a beautiful hot sunny day, such a nice setting with the mountains and Air Force One as the backdrop. This was my first time to see Air Force One fly in.

I had never seen anything like the anticipation and high energy awaiting his grand entrance. AC/DC's Thunderstruck blared while everyone waited with their phones up to record the moment President Trump stepped off Air Force One.

Earlier, Fred Keller had spoken; his election was the next day, and he won by 70 percent. Donald Trump Jr. also gave a very good speech, and he did autographs and pictures for the people who were in front at the barricade.

President Trump came out to the crowd cheering, "USA, USA, USA!" "Hello, Pennsylvania. I am thrilled to be back in the state that gave us American independence." It was very hot during President Trump's speech, and four people fainted, but they ended up fine, so that was a relief.

This was my favorite rally so far. It was perfect: the weather, no VIP in front of us, and I got to see Air Force One for the first time. At the conclusion of the rally, I went onto the bleachers to get some up-close pictures of Air Force One. The post rally meal came from Sheetz, a popular stop for travelers. I arrived home the following day.

## Rally #28 – Orlando, Florida 6/18/2019

This rally was announced almost three weeks in advance, so everyone had time to make plans to be there. I hadn't been to Disney World or Sea World in a while, so I decided to go early and make it a vacation.

At this rally, President Trump would be announcing his second-term presidential run with First Lady Melania, Vice President Mike Pence, and Second Lady Karen Pence at the 20,000 seat Amway Center.

I arrived at the rally on Monday morning. A line had already formed, as people arrived forty-two hours early. When I got there, the line was moving away from the front of the venue and over to a side street. I put my chair over there along the fence line.

By nighttime, there were blocks of people camping out in tents. At 8:00 a.m., they opened up the gate; we were lined up near, and the first 8,000 people lined up in there. It was nice in there, with music and food trucks. The idea was to use that as a holding area for 8,000 people at a time. When we were out and into the venue, the next 8,000 people would be let into the holding area.

During the couple of days in line, we experienced some storms with thunder and lightning. As the time got closer to the venue opening, downpours of rain would come and go. We stayed dry, though, under a canopy. When I got down to the floor area, about ten feet from the usual standing area, the volunteers stood with their arms locked.

About fifteen minutes later, the volunteers said, "Go," so that created a short stampede. Everyone was smashed together. Finally, some people moved back a bit to make some room. I had never seen so much media at a rally. They had the usual large stage, but many tables and chairs were set up behind that area.

Just after President Trump took the stage, he said he was thrilled to be back in his second home, the great state of Florida. "The American dream is back, bigger and better and stronger than ever before. By the way, that's a lot of fake news back there. The amount of press looks like the Academy Awards before it went down the tubes."

After the rally, I decided to walk thirty-five minutes to the Wawa to get some food. A white truck pulled up and said, "Do you want to get in?" I said, "No, I don't know you." He said, "You better because you are in a very bad neighborhood." So, I got a ride to the Wawa and was dropped off at my hotel. I got a Lyft to the airport early the next morning, flew out of Orlando, and was back home the next evening.

President Donald Trump raked in $24.8 million in cam-paign contributions for his re-election effort in less than twenty-four hours. Enthusiasm across the country for this president was unlike anything we had ever seen.

After days of speculation and optimistic statements by the two leaders, President Trump and North Korean leader Kim Jong Un met and shook hands on Sunday, June 30, 2019, at the Demilitarized Zone between North and South Korea.

Trump became the first US sitting president to step foot inside the Hermit Kingdom. "I was proud to step over the line," Trump told Kim later, "Inside the Freedom House on the South Korea side," according to the Associated Press, "It is a great day for the world."

On June 19, 2019, the Trump administration announced plans for a unique July 4 celebration in Washington, DC. President Trump would deliver a speech from the Lincoln Memorial as part of a series of day-long events that included a military-themed parade near the National Mall and flyovers featuring planes used for Air Force One. It would be called the Salute to America.

I headed to the airport early on July 2. The plane needed maintenance, so I ended up leaving three hours late. I finally got to Washington, DC, at 4:00 p.m. instead of noon. I checked into the Grand Hyatt, which was in a location that was close to the areas I would be visiting. I walked around the Lincoln Memorial to see what the setup would be like. After that, I saw the Unity Bridge parked at Harry's Restaurant. I went in there to eat and saw many people I knew.

The next day, I went to Trump International for a working lunch. I spent several hours there planning future events that I would attend. That evening, I attended an event at Harry's Restaurant. It was a nice event with speakers and a buffet. Later in the evening, new signs were put up around the Lincoln Memorial area. It looked like the general admission would be way back, too far to see much of anything.

Then, it was the morning of July 4. Instead of being very far back, I started calling the boat cruises for viewing fireworks, as I thought that would be easier. I had a reservation for the Spirit of Washington of Mt. Vernon fireworks cruise. It was $400 and included a buffet. The cruise left the dock at 6:30 p.m. and returned at 10:30 p.m.

I watched the parade at the corner of 17th Street and Constitution Avenue. The parade went by my location from 11:45 a.m. to 2:00 p.m. It was a very hot day, around ninety degrees. I walked over near the White House after to purchase some water as all of the beverages had sold out.

When I entered the table area for the boat cruise, I discovered that my seat was at a table right by the window.

It was a very nice cruise with a delicious buffet. I watched President Donald Trump's speech on RSBN on my phone. This was a successful trip with so many things to see and do. I left early the next morning and was home by afternoon.

## Rally #29 – Greenville, North Carolina 7/17/2019

On July 2, it was announced that President Trump would hold a rally in Greenville, North Carolina. I flew out of Detroit with a stop in Charlotte to arrive at 11:30 p.m. I got some food at the Sheetz and joined the line around midnight. At around 4:00 a.m., the line moved into the maze of barricades. We were able to have our chairs in there and get food from one of the many food trucks. The temperature reached 107 degrees, so I had mint ice cream to keep cool.

The line stayed organized the whole day. I was able to get my usual spot near the podium. This time, there was a double barricade, so that meant there would be VIP placed in front of us at the last minute. It worked out well, as there were no tall people blocking our view. Before the rally started, the 8,000 seats were full, and there were many people outside not able to get in. Since the overflow crowds continued to grow, a jumbotron was set outside of the rally for viewing.

After the rally, I had a meal at Denny's. While I was there, a lady liked my shirt and gave me thirty dollars for my meal. I had some delicious nachos. After eating, I stayed at the airport to catch an early morning flight home.

On July 24, 2019, it was stated that Robert Mueller's hearing was a disaster for the Democrats and the reputation of Robert Mueller.

Former Special Council Mueller appeared in front of the House Judiciary Committee on July 24 to testify on his finalized report and the Trump administration's alleged collusion with Russia.

During Mueller's testimony, he constantly asked for questions to be repeated, seemed unsure of his answers, and forgot to speak into the microphone.

Mueller seemed to be forgetting his own work, and at one point, contradicted his own report, only to agree with it minutes later. "The Democrats had nothing, and now they have less than nothing." President Trump said, following the Mueller testimony.

On July 27, 2019, President Trump had some harsh, arguably true things to say about Baltimore. In a controversial tweet, the president said, "Cummings' district is a disgusting rat and rodent infested mess."

Republican activist Scott Presler stepped to the plate to tackle the issue head-on. On July 28, he tweeted: "Next week, I am coming to Baltimore. I am organizing a trash cleanup in the city." This was met with an enormous outpouring of support from his followers and thousands of other Trump supporters online. The cleanup was on August 5, and anyone could sign up for a shift to come help out. More than 170 people came from around the country and cleaned up nearly twelve tons of trash.

In August 2019, fundraisers netted Trump $12 million for re-election. President Trump appeared at two Hamptons fundraisers organized by Trump Victory. I wanted to attend one of these, as they had a low-end ticket for $2800, which was very affordable. I was going to go with a friend of mine, but we never found out the proper address for the event, so we didn't make it. It would have been great; no hotel was needed as these were luncheons.

On August 15, 2019, there was a rally scheduled in Manchester, New Hampshire. I missed this rally because I was in a different Manchester. I had headed over to Manchester UK for an Ed Sheeran concert. I remember this moment like it was yesterday. I landed in Newark, New Jersey. I traveled through the mountains of Pennsylvania after attending the Ed Sheeran concert in the United Kingdom.

I listened to BBC Radio, and they explained the situation taking place in Hong Kong. I had seen a little bit about it in the news, but did not have the full story.

This is what I learned. Hong Kong, a former British colony in Southeastern China, had enjoyed a special status under the principle, "One country, two systems." Basic law dictated that Hong Kong would retain its common law in capitalist system for fifty years after the handover in 1997. What this meant was that Hong Kong could keep its freedom until 2047.

China had been chipping away at Hong Kong's freedom and system of government. The people of Hong Kong were finally fed up and started protesting. After hearing all of this, I knew I had to go. Someone from the United States needed to show Hong Kong that we supported them. The peaceful protests were always on a Sunday, which they called Family Day. I did some research and discovered I could fly to Hong Kong for $999.00, and I would only be gone for the weekend. That sounded great, so I booked the flights.

It turned out to be a crazy day at the airports, and I almost did not make it. I sat on the runway in Detroit for three hours, so that meant I missed my flight from

Chicago to San Francisco. Upon arriving to Chicago, I got a different flight to San Francisco. But when I got to San Francisco, my flight to Hong Kong had already left. This was very time sensitive, as they are twelve hours ahead, and I needed to be there all day Sunday. As it turned out, there was a flight from San Francisco to Taiwan to Hong Kong.

Upon landing in Taiwan, I heard my name paged. Someone put me on an earlier flight to Hong Kong right away. I ended up landing at 9:00 p.m. on Saturday night on September 14, 2019. I took a taxi to the Hotel Icon. It was a beautiful hotel and had a fridge stocked with free snacks. I watched Fox News for a while and watched scenes of the Hong Kong protest.

The next morning, I took a train to Chater Garden, which was close to a mall. I saw someone carrying the British flag, so I followed him, which led to the British Consulate. There was a large gathering of people there holding signs and British flags. They were chanting, "Fight for freedom" and "One country, two systems, is dead." They had an envelope with their five demands, and someone came out to receive it. The first peaceful protest lasted from noon to 1:15 p.m. I was told to go to Victoria Park, which was two stops away by train. People would be gathering there by 2:00 p.m. for a peaceful protest march.

When I arrived at this area, it reminded me of New York City. The streets were wide, and there were many skyscrapers. I noticed a large group of people holding American flags, so I headed over there. Some of the protesters were holding a banner that said, "President Trump, Please Liberate Hong Kong." I pulled out the Donald Trump Keep America Great Flag 2020. They liked that, and escorted me right up to the front of the group.

I pulled out another one for them to use, along with a lot of American flags.

They had me lead the peaceful protest march down the middle of the streets of Hong Kong while they chanted, "Fight for freedom" and "President Trump, please liberate Hong Kong." The march lasted from 2:30 p.m. to 4:30 p.m. and ended with them singing the National Anthem.

Normally, by 6:00 p.m., everyone leaves because all of the trains are shut down to capture the protesters. I could not get back to the hotel. A girl told me to follow her, and she led me to a big ferry boat. She handed me some tokens, and I boarded just in time. It was a twenty-minute boat ride with the passengers singing during the ride.

I had just enough time to stop at McDonald's, pick up my luggage, and shuttle to the airport. The trip home went smoothly. It was from Hong Kong to Seoul and South Korea to Detroit. I left Seoul at 10:35 a.m. and arrived at Detroit at 10:00 a.m. due to the time difference. Hong Kong is twelve hours ahead. It was a successful journey in which I learned a lot. Mainly, I learned that maybe what you see on television isn't what is really happening. And that is what I discovered.

On September 27, 2019, President Trump and Indian Prime Minister Narendra Modi exchanged warm words of friendship in Houston at a rare mass rally for a foreign leader. Approximately 50,000 people attended the "Howdy, Modi!" event, which President Trump called a historic event. Greeted by a standing ovation, President Trump praised Mr. Modi, who he said was doing an exceptional job for India.

### Rally #30 – Dallas, Texas 10/17/2019

The Trump campaign announced that President Trump would hold a rally at the American Airlines Arena in Dallas, Texas. "President Trump looks forward to celebrating the good news of the Trump economy and the vast accomplishments of his administration with the great men and women of Texas."

I flew out of Lansing, Michigan, with a stop in Chicago, to then arrive in Dallas at 8:00 p.m. When I arrived at the venue, I saw people I knew, so I got in line with them. The line was on the sidewalk of a busy downtown intersection. There was a 7-Eleven at the corner that had delicious food and was open twenty-four hours. It was a cold and windy night, but I always seem to get a good night's sleep right on the pavement.

The next day, they were holding a Women's Fair at the Plaza right near our line. It was fun to look at all the booths and participate in a free yoga class. Later that day, I went to dinner with a lady I met in line. We went to the Spaghetti Warehouse. I had been there many years ago. This was an Italian restaurant with delicious food. I felt like I had gone back in time as they sat me in the same booth that I had sat in years ago. The section we sat in was an old railroad car. After eating, we headed to the line for the event.

The lines going into this rally were confusing as they used many entrances to get in. When I got to the podium area, I chose to stand at the right side because the sides were single barricades and the middle was double barricades. That way, you were sure you would see, as no one would be in front of you. As usual, it was a great rally with Ted Cruz, Ivanka, and Jared in attendance.

By the time I finally got to the airport, the security was closed, so I had to sleep on the floor on the boring side of the airport. Before entering the rally, I hid my small pillow and blanket in some long grass, but it was gone when I got out, which is rare. But I was fine at the airport without them. The next morning, I left at 8:00 a.m. and had a stop in Chicago, so I was able to buy some of their delicious pizza. Then it was time to board the final plane to home.

On October 27, 2019, President Trump announced that Abu Bakr al-Baghdadi, the elusive Islamic State commander, died during US military operation in Syria. "Last night, the United States brought the world's number one terrorist leader to justice. He was a sick and depraved man, and now he is gone."

Trump praised his military and intelligence officials for the operation, which he said he watched from the White House Situation Room on Saturday evening.

On December 10, 2019, Democrats announced they would introduce two articles of impeachment, making clear that they intended to charge President Donald Trump with abuse of power in an obstruction of Congress. President Trump said the impeachment was a "Witch Hunt," which it was.

## Rally #31 – Battle Creek, Michigan 12/18/2019

On December 5, 2019, it was announced that President Trump would hold a "Merry Christmas" rally at Battle Creek Arena on December 18, 2019. I drove to Battle Creek, Michigan, on December 16 and arrived at 1:00 p.m. Upon arrival to the venue, a building inspector was there, so the two of us walked around inside to see what the setup would be like. There was a parking garage attached and a Bixby's, which was open for business.

My friend arrived a bit later, and we went to Clara's Restaurant; it was an old train depot and was very busy due to people having Christmas parties there.

After dinner, we got in our individual vehicles to sleep for the night. In the morning, we were able to purchase a five-dollar parking pass for the day. Then we decided to start the line. A local radio station wanted us to call in for an interview. After doing these interviews, people stopped by to visit us. A real nice man brought us some delicious soup from Horrocks, as it was a cold day, but at least the sun was shining.

A short time later, people joined us in line. Some local people provided food for the first group of people in the line. They brought ten pizzas, pop, coffee, and donuts in the morning.

As evening approached, it got colder, but we were told we could move the line into the parking garage. So that is where everyone set up sleeping bags, tents, and chairs. This would be where we would enter the venue, so it was nice not having to move again the next day. During the night, we got four to five inches of snow, so it was nice to have spent the night indoors.

The day of the rally always goes by fast. We entered the rally at 2:00 p.m. I decided to stand in front of the podium for this one. The rally started late due to waiting for the impeachment vote. President Trump spoke for two hours and ten minutes. This was a good rally, no last-minute line cutters, and most importantly, a single barricade. Most of the people I knew at this rally had a short distance to drive home. I stayed in a hotel and drove home the next morning.

# Chapter 5

# January 2020 to June 2020

——— ★ ———

### Rally #32 – Toledo, Ohio 1/9/2020

On December 23, 2019, the Trump campaign announced that it would hold its first 2020 campaign rally in Toledo, Ohio. The "Keep America Great" rally would take page on January 9, 2020, at the Huntington Center.

I left for this rally by car since it wasn't a long drive. I met up with some friends at the Port Lawrence parking garage. We set up our chairs in front of the venue the day before the rally. It was a cold and windy day, much colder than the previous rally in Battle Creek, Michigan.

By dinner time, the line had grown, so the rally-goers took turns getting something to eat while the others would watch the chairs. I went to the Spaghetti Warehouse. I got the Wednesday night special, which consisted of spaghetti, salad, and bread for $5.36.

We headed back after dinner to spend the night in line. I borrowed a tent to stay in while many others slept in sleeping bags and chairs. OAN Network did a short video they posted on Twitter. President Trump retweeted the video, so I later saw the tent I was in online.

In the morning, someone showed up with donuts for the first group of people in line. This happened often at the rallies. The local people would show up to support the people in line with food, water, blankets, and anything else that was needed.

This rally was very well organized on the outside. Barricades were set up in front of the venue very early, so the line formed between those. This was nice because it stopped groups of people from standing around the venue to cut in when the doors opened. There were also four food trucks across the street.

The doors opened just after 1:00 p.m. Upon entering this one, we were told we had to go upstairs and maze through the seats to get to the floor area, instead of just walking across the floor right where we came in. This was quickly changed, as it didn't make sense to do that. So, after mazing through the seats, I chose a standing spot in front of the podium. It was another great setup with only one barricade.

During the rally, President Trump celebrated his decision to order a drone strike, killing the Iranian commander, Qassim Suleimani, calling him the world's top terrorist. "He was a blood-thirsty terror, and he is no longer a terror. He is dead."

"I see the radical left Democrats have expressed outrage over the termination of this horrible terrorist," he said. "And you know, instead, they should be outraged by Suleimani's savage crimes."

At the conclusion of this rally, the sidewalk and streets were very congested. It took over thirty minutes to walk the short distance to the parking garage. I was then at my home. It was another successful rally, as the waiting in line was worth it when there was a single barricade.

On Wednesday, January 15, 2020, President Trump signed the first stage of a US-China agreement that represented a truce in the long-running trade war, calling it "A great deal for both countries."

Also on January 15, 2020, the House formally delivered articles of impeachment against President Donald Trump, triggering a Senate trial to start the next day. Speaker Nancy Pelosi had a signing ceremony Wednesday evening, hours after the House passed a resolution to send the articles to the other side of the Capitol and appoint the Democrats hand-picked team of impeachment managers.

President Donald Trump addressed the annual March for Life on January 24, telling Pro-Life demonstrators that he was an advocate for the right to life of unborn children and calling for a federal prohibition on late-term abortion. He is the first president to attend the march in person, which began in 1974, and has become one of the largest annual political events in the country.

### Rally #33 – Wildwood, New Jersey 1/28/2020

As soon as this rally was announced, I made plans to attend. It took place in New Jersey, a state in which I had never attended a rally before. My goal was to see President Trump speak in as many different states as possible. I would not always pick the closest state to travel to. For example, if he had two rallies in the same day, and the closest rally was in a state I had seen him speak before, then instead, I would travel further to see him in a new state.

Many of the hotel owners were shocked, as many of the hotels sold out within twelve hours of the rally being announced. Many of the local businesses that were normally closed re-opened for several days for this event. It was stated that approximately 100,000 tickets were requested for the rally at the Wildwoods Convention Center, which could hold up to 7,400 people.

Early in the morning on January 27, 2020, I flew on Spirit out of Detroit with a stop in Ft. Myers to land in Atlantic City. It was fifty-one miles from Wildwood, so I took a ninety-one dollar Lyft.

The line had formed a couple of blocks from the convention center. I decided to walk around the area, as I had never been there before. This would be a great place to visit in the summer. I walked along the 2.5 mile boardwalk. There was a nice beach and many shops.

After returning to the line, very shortly, the staff walked the line into the barricaded area into the venue. This would be the lineup to enter the venue the next day. By 6:00 p.m., there were at least 1,200 people in line. Thankfully, the hotel across the street dropped off blankets for the people at the front of the line. Many of the businesses went all out in support of President Trump's upcoming rally. There were Trump signs, billboards, and banners. I had never seen anything like it.

By morning, the line was so long that you could clearly tell people in the back would not get in. But they had the jumbotron set up outside for the overflow crowd. When it was time to go in, I got through the security quickly and headed right to the podium area. No one else came in. I was the only one inside. Finally, people were let in. The staff had let a couple of people through security and were told to hold them back in the lobby area, as it wasn't time to go in yet.

And as usual, when President Trump took the stage, the crowd went wild. "I love New Jersey, and I am thrilled to be back in the Garden State." After the rally, some people took us to a delicious Italian meal at Duffinetti's Restaurant. After a late dinner, I took the last bus to Atlantic City. It was too dangerous to stay at the bus terminal, so I walked to the Caesar's Palace Casino just to have a place to lay around to then take a Lyft to the airport. I was home by early evening.

On February 4, 2020, Donald Trump made his third State of the Union address, "The Great American Comeback." This was one of my favorite parts of his speech:

> America is a place where anything can happen. America is a place where anyone can rise. Here, on this land, on this soil, on this continent, the most incredible dreams come true. This nation is our canvas. And this country is our masterpiece. We look at tomorrow and see limited frontiers just waiting to be explored. Our brightest discoveries are not yet known. Our most thrilling stories are not yet told. Our grandest journeys are not yet made. The American age, the American epic, the American adventure, has only just begun. Our spirit is still young. The sun is still rising. God's grace is still shining. My fellow Americans, the best is yet to come.

During the last few seconds of President Trump's State of the Union address, Nancy Pelosi ripped up the President's speech behind his back. She later defended her actions, stating that it was a collection of false statements. Soon after the State of the Union address, I got on Amazon and searched for a "Best Is Yet to Come" t-shirt to wear at an upcoming rally.

On September 6, 2020, President Trump proudly held up the USA Today with the headlines, "Acquitted," at a Thursday morning national prayer breakfast. It was his first appearance since he was declared not guilty in the Senate impeachment trial. He later made some remarks from the East Room. Mitt Romney was the lone Republican to vote guilty as the door closed on the impeachment saga.

**Rally #34 – Manchester, New Hampshire 2/10/2020**

On January 23, 2020, the Trump campaign announced that President Trump would hold a "Keep America Great" rally at the SNHU Arena in Manchester, New Hampshire on February 10, 2020. As soon as this rally was announced, I knew I would be going, as it was a new state for me to attend a rally. This would be my thirty-fourth rally in seventeen different states.

I arrived at the Lansing airport early in the afternoon. As the day went on, the snow came down harder; it was so bad that I could barely see out the airport windows. As time went on, I was told the flight would be late, and I would miss my connection in Washington, DC. I was then told they would shuttle us to Detroit ninety-three miles. Then everyone could keep their cars in Lansing and keep their return flights.

By 7:00 p.m. I realized that would not happen, as they said it was too dangerous to be on the roads. They told me to drive to Detroit and call while driving to get the one flight from Detroit to Manchester.

When I got into the car and started driving, it was a terrible blizzard. It was very difficult to keep the car on the road. I could not go much faster than 45 mph. I saw many cars slide into the deep ditches on both sides. There was a pile-up of three semi-trucks, and at one point, I saw a semi-truck deep in the woods. After two hours of extremely stressful driving, I made it just in time to board the plane to Manchester. I arrived at Manchester and took a short Lyft ride to the venue. I joined the line; it was snowing and raining off and on all night.

By 7:00 a.m., the staff moved us close to the venue, and a line was formed between the barricades. Upon entering the venue, I had to go upstairs and maze through the seats to find an open aisle leading to the floor area. This was a single barricade, so I chose to be right in front of the podium.

There were a lot of speakers at this rally, as it was President Trump's first rally since his acquittal. Kimberly Guilfoyle and Donald Trump Jr. both spoke. "I am thrilled to be back in the great state of New Hampshire. We have more people outside than we do inside, but the fake news will not report it. They just show my face."

I saw President Trump pull a paper out of his suit jacket. He said, "People have been requesting The Snake. Have any of you heard it?" My friend and I raised our hands, and he said, "I know you two have. Look at those front-row people; they are warriors, like my congressmen. I used to do this a lot, and people could not get enough of it. We don't want open borders. This is called The Snake." It always got so quiet when he read this poem about illegal immigration. "You knew damn well I was a snake before you let me in."

After the rally, I had some delicious nachos at Murphy's Tap Room. I arrived at the airport at 4:00 a.m. I happened to be standing near the airline staff and heard her get a message that the staff did not show up to fly the plane. They said the flight could not go due to maintenance, and that was the only one of the day. I ended up with a new ticket, from Boston to Detroit with a thirty-minute wait in LaGuardia.

The staff said they would shuttle us to Boston. I was thinking as time went by, "I bet that will never happen." I found two people sitting around and said, "I think we should split a Lyft to Boston."

It was a stressful ride as there wasn't a lot of time to make the flight, and we were in morning rush hour traffic. We successfully completed the fifty-five-mile ride and got to our gates on time. My layover in Boston was supposed to be for thirty minutes. It turned out to be a two-minute layover. Wow, what a relief to finally be heading toward home, or so I thought.

I experienced rough turbulence on this flight; at one point, my cup of juice flew straight up into the air, and I was able to grab the cup in mid-air and catch the juice without having it spill. They announced that we were in a holding pattern. We approached Gate C3, and thankfully, I was flying out of C1.

I could see the plane still sitting there and was hoping it would not take off before I boarded. During this time, the de-planing process seemed to take forever. I always travel light, so I got to the front area and made it to C1 quickly and was the last one to board. When I arrived at Detroit, I had to get a shuttle to the parking garage since I ended up on American Airlines flying out and Delta flying in. Wow, what a journey.

I had a roundtrip ticket to Manchester, New Hampshire, from Lansing and purchased a new roundtrip ticket for coming home, and none of the tickets were used, as obstacles kept me from doing so. Thankfully, everything worked out, but it wasn't easy.

## Rally #35 – Phoenix, Arizona 2/19/2020

On February 10, 2020, it was announced that President Trump would hold a rally in Phoenix, Arizona, at the Arizona Veterans Memorial Coliseum on February 19. I started planning to be at this one, as it would be my eighteenth different state.

It was a dangerous drive to Chicago O'Hare Airport. Just like before, cars were spinning out and into the deep ditches. There were accidents all over, as people were not slowing down in these very bad conditions. It was a relief to finally get the car parked at the airport at 2:30 a.m. This would be my first time flying on Frontier, which was from Chicago to Phoenix.

I arrived at the rally the day before, secured a spot in line, and headed to lunch. I ate at Mel's Diner. It was known for its exterior being filmed in the television series *Alice*. At this venue, there was a large gate that was locked, so the line formed there for the night. In the morning, the line moved closer to the venue. After going through security, there was a ramp that entered into the building. I entered the venue at the top area of seats and mazed down to the floor area to get close to the podium.

I had a good spot to view the rally, especially since there was only one barricade, meaning no one would be in the front blocking my view. This was the first rally where

I wore my "The Best Is Yet to Come" t-shirt. It was a black t-shirt with white letters.

Kimberly Guilfoyle and Donald Trump Jr. spoke at this rally. President Trump concluded his speech with "The Best is yet to come" and "Make America great again." Toward the end of the rally, I noticed Kimberly and Don Jr. standing in the back stage area at an entrance. They noticed my "Best Is Yet to Come" shirt, and were waving, pointing, and clapping. They came over and shook hands with many people at the conclusion of the rally.

I stopped at Denny's, which was close to the airport, and stayed there all night. In the morning, I got a Lyft to the airport. It was a good flight home without any incidents for a change.

On February 24, 2020, President Trump and First Lady Melania Trump traveled 8,000 miles to deliver a message: America loves India. It was a political-style rally like no other. Even Trump's MAGA rallies couldn't compare to the size and scope of the "Namaste Trump" rally, which was held in Motera Stadium with a capacity of 110,000. As Trump's motorcade made its way to the stadium, the Indian music gave way to Trump's playlist, including Macho Man and Tiny Dancer.

"Trump's visit is a new chapter in the relationship between the US and India; a chapter that will document the progress and prosperity of Americans and Indians, Modi said in Hindi."

## CPAC 2020

I had never been to the Conservative Political Action Conference, and decided I would go that year. It was held at the Gaylord National Resort and Conference Center in

National Harbor, Maryland. I had a round-trip flight from Lansing to DC with a stop in Detroit. The plane left thirty minutes late due to de-icing, and once again, I was the last one to board in Detroit.

I got to the convention at 9:00 a.m. and was able to check in right away. The rooms were nice with a balcony that looked over the atrium. I listened to the speakers all day and ate at a restaurant on site. I listened to the speakers all day on Friday and was going out to dinner at Trump International, but it was sold out to reservations only.

On Saturday at 1:30 a.m., I got in line to get into the large conference room that President Trump would speak at Saturday evening. The line had formed at 10:00 p.m., so there were about fifty people ahead of me. At 6:00 a.m., they moved the line through a large room, and at that point, you had to compare your ID with your badge. After this, it was fast walking to the TSA.

The doors opened at 7:00 a.m., and I got the closest row I could in general admission. There were speakers all day where speakers at different events were highlighted. They highlighted the peaceful protest march that I was at in Hong Kong.

President Trump was supposed to speak by late afternoon, but instead, he did a live press conference from the White House from 3:40–5:10 p.m., and then he came over for his CPAC speech. By this time, I had already missed my flight home but was able to catch a ride by car to the airport in Lansing, where my car was.

I really enjoyed my first CPAC Conference. It was nice to listen to many different speakers all in one venue with the hotel and restaurants attached. Little did I know that this would be the last public event I would attend for several months.

## Coronavirus

On January 9, 2020, the World Health Organization announced a mysterious coronavirus in Wuhan, China.

On January 21, 2020, a Washington State resident became the first person in the United States with a confirmed case.

On January 29, 2020, the White House started its Coronavirus Response Task Force, headed by US Health and Human Services Secretary Alex Azar.

On January 30, 2020, the World Health Organization issued a global health emergency. At that time, the death toll was over more than 200 and at least 9,800 cases.

On January 31, 2020, President Trump issued an executive order blocking entry to the US from China.

On February 3, 2020, the Trump administration declared a public health emergency due to the coronavirus outbreak.

On March 6, 2020, twenty-one people tested positive on a cruise ship off the coast of California.

On March 11, 2020, President Trump banned travel from Europe, which saw cases increase in Italy and Spain.

On March 13, 2020, President Trump declared COVID-19 a national emergency, which unblocked billions of dollars in federal funding to fight the disease's spread.

On March 17, 2020, President Trump asked everyone to work from home if possible and postpone unnecessary travel.

On March 17, 2020, the administration asked Congress to send Americans direct financial relief checks to Americans as part of an economic stimulus package.

On March 19, 2020, California became the first state to issue a stay-at-home order mandating all residents to stay at home except to go to an essential job or shop for essential needs.

On March 21, 2020, the Canada-US border closed to all but essential travel.

On March 27, 2020, President Trump signed the CARES Act into law. It was the largest economic recovery package in history. It would provide direct payments to Americans and expansions of unemployment insurance.

On April 4, 2020, President Trump said that the US citizen should try an anti-malaria drug, hydroxychloroquine, to treat COVID-19.

In Michigan, the stay-at-home order went into effect on March 24 and would supposedly stay in effect until April 13. But the stay-at-home order in Michigan was extended four times and lasted seventy days with ever-changing restrictions.

Many residents of Michigan opposed the governor's restrictions, stating she was placing a gridlock on Michigan's economy. They stated they were tired of living in lockdown and wanted to get back to work because the stay-at-home order was ruining their livelihood.

A protest was planned for April 15, 2020, at noon in downtown Lansing, Michigan. The protest organizers called it "Operation Gridlock," their response to what they saw as the governor unnecessarily placed a gridlock on society. Thousands of protectors showed up in Lansing to show their opposition to Whitmer's extended stay-at-home order.

On Wednesday afternoon, traffic on Allegan Street was at a standstill, and the Capitol building was heavily congested with protestors. This was just one of the protests that happened at the state capital in spring 2020.

On May 20, 2020, protest was called "Operation Haircut." The event was held in opposition that hair salons and barber shops remain closed. Barbers and hairstylists offered free haircuts in front of the capitol.

I noticed many new signs up at local businesses in town. "The demand for this product is extraordinarily high" was posted where toilet paper and paper towels used to be stocked. Many stores announced they would no longer be open twenty-four hours. I saw this sign on the floor, "Thank you for practicing social distancing, please keep at least six feet apart." I saw these signs at a couple stores, "We are unable to accept cans or bottles during this time," and "Drinking fountains are closed until further notice."

The fitness centers, barber shops, and hair salons were closed until further notice. Many items were limited to one per person, such as: toilet paper, paper towels, hand sanitizer, sanitizing aerosols, dish soap, and so forth.

On April 17, 2020, President Trump's re-election campaign said they still planned to hold rallies leading up to the November election.

In May 2020, it was announced that President Donald Trump planned on visiting Mt. Rushmore to see the fireworks on July 3, 2020. In the past, the fireworks were not allowed due to environmental reasons. Governor Kristi Noem tweeted: "This year, we're bringing fireworks back to Mt. Rushmore to celebrate Independence Day. Great news @realDonaldTrump is coming to enjoy the show with us."

After the death of George Floyd, riots and arson left Minnesota communities devastated. The protests continued from July to October in other major cities, including Portland and Seattle. Many of the demonstrations involved rioting and heated confrontations with law enforcement. I did not attend any of them.

The Trump campaign announced that President Trump would hold a rally in Tulsa, Oklahoma, on June 19, 2020. It would be the first rally since the coronavirus pandemic.

## Rally #36 – Tulsa, Oklahoma June 20, 2020

As soon as this rally was announced, I decided I would attend because it would be my 19th state to see a rally. It was originally scheduled on Juneteenth, but was changed to June 20. I had already purchased my airline ticket and was supposed to come home on Saturday, so that had to be changed.

I started out on this journey on June 16, not knowing that this road trip would seem to never end. My flight was with American Airlines Detroit to Tulsa with a short stop in Dallas. I thought the airline would not be busy and they would do what they said on the news. They did not do any health screening, the middle seats were full, it wasn't at 60 percent capacity, as the only empty seat was the one next to me. It was also stated that the passengers in the back aisles would enter first; that did not happen either.

Upon entering the plane, a water bottle, snack, and a plastic bag were handed to each passenger. I arrived at the BOK Center by Lyft on the afternoon of June 17. Soon after I arrived, I did a short interview with a local Fox affiliate, finding out later that this was aired on Fox, CNN, and my local news at home, which turned into a nightmare. This was my last in-person interview at a rally, as this one stirred up too much trouble.

The time, waiting in line went by fast, as there was always something nearby to see or do. The local residents brought in donuts, breakfast sandwiches, bags of snacks, and coolers full of ice, which they replenished daily with pop, Gatorade, and water. At some point each day, they would drop off a large stack of pizzas.

The first night I was there, the line had formed in front of the BOK Center on the sidewalk. For this one, people used sleeping bags, tents, and cots. On Thursday evening, all of a sudden, hundreds of Ford Mustangs did a parade in front of the BOK Center. It was fun to watch; some of the people in line flew large Trump flags in the street near the cars.

After the parade, we found out that the line would move to a different location, Cheyenne and Fourth. After moving the line, the mayor announced a 10:00 p.m. curfew. We were allowed to stay outside in line on the sidewalk but could not wander around. I woke up at 3:00 a.m. to loud banging noises. They put up nine-foot fences all around the venue area, which covered many large blocks. This would be called the "Sterile Zone."

On Friday, I walked around the Sterile Zone to see which way would be the quickest to get to the venue. I saw there was a large stage set up where Clay Walker would play on Saturday afternoon before the rally. By 10:00 a.m., everyone stood in the middle of the street, and the front of the line was right at the big fence. They let a few people in at a time.

First, you proceeded to the health screening area and were handed a mask. After that, it was time to walk through the aisles of barricades. The next step was temperature checks, then security check through the magnetometers. After completing this, it was time to run to the venue. It actually looked like a marathon with everyone running through the streets with people on the sidelines cheering.

It was very hot and at least 3/4 of a mile to the venue. When I arrived at the BOK Center, the barricades were set up, and that is where everyone went to form the line to enter the venue. While we waited in line, we listened to Clay Walker perform on a large stage that was set up outside.

When I finally got down to the floor area of the venue, it was very crowded. I was able to get a spot in front of the podium.

Just before President Trump was to come on stage, I received a message that people at home had seen my interview and were making extremely hateful comments, stating I would come home and spread the virus all over. I never did read the comments. I just figured it was easier to ignore the haters, as I didn't have time for arguing back and forth. And guess what, this is what ended up happening.

Thank goodness I was safe and sound at a rally in Tulsa, Oklahoma, because at home at the commons area of my apartment complex, a religious event was held, and at that event, some people tested positive for COVID-19.

President Trump came out and said, "I want to thank you. You are warriors. We had some very bad people out-side." I later found out some protestors had destroyed the health screening area so no one else could get in, as you had to be screened to be inside the venue. Also, after the rally, I didn't see any violence either. It was a short walk to the hotel, and the police and National Guard were there protecting the area.

On Sunday morning, I thought I had a ride to the next rally in Phoenix, Arizona, which was approximately six-teen hours away. The ride did not work out well. I found myself stranded in Albuquerque, New Mexico. The plan

THE BEST IS YET TO COME...

was to rent a car in New Mexico, drive six hours to Phoenix, Arizona, for the Students for Trump event on June 23, then drive 4.5 hours to Las Vegas, to fly home on the 24th.

I started walking along Route 66 in ninety-degree heat, pulling my suitcase for 2.5 miles to get a bus to the rental car place. I had ordered a small car online, but when I got there, they said they needed this 2020 Cadillac Escalade dropped off in Las Vegas, and it would be the same price. I made it to the Dream City Church in Phoenix, Arizona.

### Rally #37 – Phoenix, Arizona 6/23/2020

This event was hosted by Charlie Kirk of Turning Point Action. The parking lot opened at 6:00 a.m., and a line formed in front of the venue. It was 109 degrees, and it took a while to get in, as at least 500 people went in first as VIP. Many of the rows of seats were reserved. I decided to go upstairs, so I was on the second level on the right side of the stage.

The venue was packed, with a capacity of 3,000. It was a very interesting event, with students speaking and Kimberly Guilfoyle, Donald Trump Jr., Charlie Kirk, and President Donald Trump spoke. After the rally, I headed to the Flamingo in Las Vegas and flew home the next morning.

# Chapter 6

# July 2020 to January 4, 2021

———— ★ ————

On July 3, President Trump headed to Mt. Rushmore in South Dakota for an early Fourth of July fireworks celebration. I decided to go since I had never been to South Dakota. I flew to Minneapolis and got a rental car. I stopped in Wall, South Dakota, and went to the famous Wall Drug. It was a nice area with many shops and restaurants.

Right after checking into my hotel in Keystone, I headed out to see Mt. Rushmore. It was so cool to be driving and then all of a sudden see it. There was a place to pull over and take pictures. I did many tourist attractions during this trip since I had headed out a few days early. I viewed the fireworks near Doane Tunnel. It was a great viewing spot. It was ninety-eight degrees, but to cool off, people walked through the tunnel. As I sat on my chair awaiting the fireworks display, I counted license plates of forty-one different states.

On July 9, I flew to Detroit to rent a car to travel to a rally in Portsmouth, New Hampshire. It started raining very hard in New York, with lightning in the distance that looked like fireworks. All of a sudden, there was an extremely loud crack of thunder, right near the car. A tree turned red as it was struck by lightning and caught on fire. This happened again, but the tree was a bit further into the woods.

When I finally arrived at Portsmouth, I found a small lineup of people that had spent the night in tents. It was getting dark and looked like rain. By 1:30 p.m. the day before the rally, I found out it was postponed due to a tropical storm coming up the east coast. The rally was scheduled to be partially outdoors in an airplane hangar at Portsmouth International Airport. It would be rescheduled at a later date.

After hearing this, it was time to travel thirteen hours back to Michigan. Upon arrival, there were no flights, so I had to wait around an additional day. The plane had mechanical issues and left about ninety minutes late. This was the only trip I made out of fifty-six rallies that ended up postponed to a later date.

On August 13, 2020, President Trump announced a historic peace agreement between Israel and United Arab Emirates. The agreement makes the UAE only the third Arab country to currently have diplomatic relations with a Jewish nation. President Trump heralded the deal as a major development for a region that had been beset by violence for decades over the issue of Israel's place in the Middle East. "By uniting two of America's closest and most capable partners in the region, something which was said could not be done, the deal is a significant step towards building a more peaceful, secure, and prosperous Middle East."

On August 18, the second night of the 2020 Democratic National Convention, the party officially nominated Joe Biden. He chose Kamala Harris to be his running mate.

## Rally #38 – Yuma, Arizona 8/18/2020

I drove to the Detroit area on August 15, 2020, to watch the MAGA Dream Cruise car parade. I had a late flight out the next day. The flight left a bit late due to a fire alarm going off. After landing in Phoenix, I rented a car to travel 2.5 hours to Yuma, Arizona. I went to the wall in Yuma, Arizona, at the Mexican border. It was exciting to be there after hearing so much about the wall. I walked right up to it and took a lot of pictures and videos. It was a very hot day with the temperatures rising between 111 and 118 degrees.

I arrived at the Joe Foss Hangar at 5:30 a.m. By 8:00 a.m., they moved the line to the convention center. A couple of hours later, the shuttle buses arrived, which drove us to the hangar.

The temperature checks were done in the air-conditioned shuttle bus. Upon exiting the shuttle, I received a wristband, mask, and hand sanitizer. As I entered the Joe Foss Hangar, the staff wanted people to go upstairs. I waiting for them to be distracted and got a chair on the floor area for this rally. They had five rows of VIP chairs. I was in row seven at the center area.

As President Trump took the stage, he thanked everyone for being there and said, "Since we caught Obama and Biden spying on my campaign, we should be entitled to another four years. You can sit down, it's 122 degrees."

"This election that we are going into is the most important election in the history of our country." Toward the end of the rally, I stood on my chair and got beautiful pictures. At this time, my neighbor saw me from the back on television. When I got home, he said, What was on your arm?" It was the orange wristband they gave us after going through the health screening.

It was a very hot thirty-minute walk back to the car after the rally. I was handed a bottle of water outside of the venue, but it was hot by the time I got to the car. It was now time to drive just over four hours to LAX for an 11:00 p.m. flight. Thankfully, I made the flight and landed in Detroit the next morning.

The Republican National Convention took place from August 24 through August 27, 2020, in Washington, DC.

I decided to be in the city where the RNC final speech was held. I had a hotel in Charlotte, North Carolina, where it was to be originally held. I then had plans to go to Jacksonville, Florida, but that was also canceled.

For this trip, I flew out of Saginaw, Michigan. It was an early flight, but after boarding, a bad thunderstorm started, and we ended up losing radio communications before taking off. After being on the runway for quite a while, they had everyone go back inside the airport.

I had to wait six hours to eventually take off for the twenty-minute flight to Detroit. Then I had an additional three-hour wait upon arrival there. I had received a fif-teen-dollar food voucher, so I used that.

When I arrived at Washington, DC, I noticed that many of the hotels were boarded up. Across the street at the CVS, they removed the large doors to replace with plywood.

On the day of the RNC, I spent some time at Trump International. I decided to watch for the motorcade twice. The first time I saw it was near Trump International, then I later saw it leaving the FEMA office.

Protesters started gathering as it got closer to the RNC speeches to begin. So, I decided to watch it on tele-vision from my hotel. After the RNC, I watched some live videos and saw Rand Paul and his wife get surrounded by a group of protesters.

I left very early the next morning and got to Detroit but was delayed there for ninety minutes due to flash floods. When I retrieved my suitcase in Saginaw, it was soaked. That had never happened before.

On August 31, 2020, Nancy Pelosi got her hair styled inside a San Francisco hair salon. This indoor hair appoint-ment violated San Francisco COVID-19 restrictions. She was seen on video not wearing a mask despite constantly lecturing everyone else to do so.

## Rally #39 – Latrobe, Pennsylvania 9/3/2020

I arrived at Arnold Palmer Regional Airport in Latrobe right before midnight. The line started the next morning. After being in line a few hours, I boarded a shuttle bus, which traveled five miles. They did the usual health screening and provided everyone with a mask and hand sanitizer. After this, I walked through the maze of barri-cades to wait entry into the hanger.

While waiting in line, it poured rain for at least three hours straight. There was no choice but to stand because the water on the ground was very deep. When I got inside the hanger, the first three rows were reserved. I sat in the center of row four. It was a great place to take pictures.

It was another successful rally. The hard part was always driving home. I would normally go as far as I could and then sleep in the car for a couple hours. I was able to make it into Michigan, rest for a while, then finish the drive home.

## Trump Labor Day Boat Parade 9/7/2020

There seemed to be a lot of boat parades taking place all across the country. I had never been to one, so I decided to attend one on Labor Day weekend.

I only had one day to get ready as I had just got home from the rally in Latrobe.

This boat parade was scheduled for September 7. It would start at Jupiter, Florida, at 11:00 a.m. and would travel southbound to Mar-a-Lago. I flew in a couple of days early to visit with other people attending this event.

The first priority was to drive by Mar-a-Lago. This was my first time to see it, and just like the pictures, I had seen it was beautiful. I took a picture of the gate. I had a great time sightseeing in the West Palm Beach and Jupiter area.

The boat I had chosen to be on for the parade was docked at Salefish Marina. We left at 9:00 a.m. and were over by the Jupiter Inlet Lighthouse by 10:30 a.m. We stayed there to watch the start of the parade and then joined in. It was a nice sunny day, ninety-two degrees.

I saw Kimberly Guilfoyle and Donald Trump Jr. go by on a large boat. There were thousands of boats in the water and many people on land and overpasses waving flags. The boats traveled down to Mar-a-Lago and returned to their individual marinas. There were many nice shops and restaurants along the marinas. I was surprised to see that these marinas were right in neighborhoods where people lived. It was such a beautiful area.

I flew home on Tuesday, and it was nice to finally have a roundtrip airfare without multiple incidents.

## Rally #40 – Freeland, Michigan 9/10/2020

This rally took place in Freeland, Michigan, at the Avflight Saginaw Hangar. The rallies were held in open-air airport hangars. They drew thousands of supporters, even when mandates were in place. President Trump characterized the rallies as "peaceful protests."

I arrived at Freeland, Michigan, the night before the rally. There was a light rain upon my arrival, and it was difficult to see where to park, as the airport roads were mazed, and some were barricaded off.

I decided to wait until daylight to get my car parked with everyone else. There were a lot of vendors selling all different kinds of Trump souvenirs at this rally. The cars were parked right near the line up to go inside. I looked for a seat that didn't have a reserved sign on it and found one near the front. At this one, I got a really good video of Air Force One coming in because I decided I would stand on the chair.

"If we win, America wins." "Tell your Governor to open up your state." "Where is Hunter?" "His first name is where." "Biden's agenda is 'Made in China,' my agenda is made in the USA."

President Trump was nominated for a Noble Peace Prize for a second time on September 11, 2020. A member of the Swedish Parliament nominated President Trump and the government of Kosovo and Serbia for the Nobel Peace Prize for their joint work for peace and economic development.

This announcement marks the second 2021 Nobel Prize nomination for President Trump. He received support from a Norwegian Parliament member over his role in brokering relations between Israel and the United Arab Emirates.

## Rally #41 – Henderson, Nevada 9/13/2020

This rally was originally scheduled at a hangar near the McCarran International Airport. Then it changed to an inside venue called Xtreme Manufacturing. At one point, it was listed as canceled. I did not know for sure that I would be going until 11:00 p.m. the night before, as I didn't want to fly out until a venue was confirmed.

When I was on the flight from Minneapolis to Las Vegas, an older male flight attendant was very loud and rude with enforcing masks. This did not affect me, as I always wore a very sheer scarf-type thing so I could breathe easy. He was going on and on. "This is not a suggestion; it's a requirement." Then he went and got a laminated page for two passengers sitting in front of me and said, "You don't want to be #321 and #322 that can't fly Delta."

The drama continued for most of the flight. The person next to me got in trouble because his mask was down. He told the flight attendant that it moved when he talked. The flight attendant told him he must tighten it. Then he said, "I'm not going to tie your mask; you are a big boy." This was a very entertaining flight, no movies required.

The Lyft app wasn't working upon landing in Las Vegas. It showed I had a Lyft coming, but they were going the wrong directions. I couldn't get it canceled to order a different one. The driver was informed, but it took a while to get the Lyft app back to the beginning. Meanwhile, a Lyft driver stepped out of his vehicle and said, "My driver canceled; who has cash?" That would be me—I got right in, and away we went. I always carry cash when traveling. It has saved me so many times.

I got dropped off at my usual spot, which is the Flamingo Hotel. This time, they had a kiosk to check in, and early check in was fifteen dollars, so I did that. They had limited capacity at the pool, so what you had to do was text them right at 10:00 a.m., and maybe you would get a text to then be able to go into the pool area. Well, at 10:00 a.m., I was still flying in, so I sent the text at 10:47 a.m. I was staying in that area in case I got a text because you only had ten minutes to arrive at the check-in point. At around 4:00 p.m., I stopped over to the check-in area to see how things were going. They were still sending out texts to the people that texted at 10:03 a.m. I knew I would not get in, but at least I knew how it worked.

I ended up with a room by the spa elevators, which I would recommend. It had a nice view of the pools and the Ferris wheel.

I walked the strip and ate at the food court near the Miracle Mile shops. Then it was time to get a Lyft to the Ahern Hotel and Convention Center for a Roger Stone event called Ungagged. I was at the table with the Bundys, the family that was famous for the Bundy Standoff. It was a standoff between supporters of cattle rancher Oliver Bundy and law enforcement.

After this, I got take-out at the Villa Kitchen in Fashion Show Mall. I got in line for the rally at around 2:30 a.m. The line was long with about 150 people. The cars were allowed to park all night in line but had to move into a neighborhood in the morning.

This line was very uncomfortable for sleeping, as I had to lie down on gravel, but I was able to make it work. In the morning, it was a half-mile walk to use a bathroom and get something to eat, as there was nothing close by. As it got closer to entry time, everyone was told to lean their chairs up against the fence and retrieve them after the rally.

It was a hot day, one hundred degrees. Being that there were about 200 people in line ahead of me, I didn't get inside until around 4:00 p.m. At this rally, fifty people were released at a time to do health screening, then lined up near the venue by walking through the barricades.

Upon entering the venue, I noticed lots of chairs, very little standing, and the cameras were way in the back. All of the front rows were reserved, so people just ended up sitting the closest they could get in the center area. I decided to walk around to the side of the stage and found a seat right at the ramp where President Trump and all the other speakers would come out to walk up to the stage.

It was a great seat, and it was super exciting to have a front-row seat to view the speakers walk out. Dana White sat just to the left of me with some other UFC fighters. As Kimberly Guilfoyle waited to come out to speak, she recognized me as I was wearing my "Best Is Yet to Come" shirt again.

After the rally, I went to Pieology to eat. It was a place where you build your own pizza. I stayed at the MGM Grand since I had an early flight in the morning, and this hotel was two miles from the airport.

When I arrived at Minneapolis, it was nice to discover that I would land at the same gate I would fly out of. I stopped at my usual restaurant at the Minneapolis Airport, Chili's. They always have delicious food. The travel home often involved three flights. I still had to fly to Detroit and then home.

## Rally #42 – Mosinee, Wisconsin 9/17/2020

It was announced that President Trump would host a Great American Comeback event in Mosinee, Wisconsin, at Central Wisconsin Aviation on September 18, 2020.

This was an easy six-hour drive, as there was not a lot of traffic. This was at a very small airport that was open twenty-four hours. I decided to park at the airport for seven dollars a day instead of going to a lot, which was free but further down the road.

I arrived at 1:00 p.m. the day before the rally and was told that we could line up near the health screening area.

We were told we had to sit in chairs all night, no camping. Well, I can't sleep very well in camp chairs, so I decided to set up my sleeping bag in this real tall grassy area. The grass and weeds were about five feet tall. I put my sleeping bag on the mulch, and when I lay down, I was surrounded by tall grass. It was perfect. I could rest, and no one would see me.

Some people sat in chairs all night, and some slept in cars. I had a great sleep there, as I usually was right down on the cement or gravel.

This rally was organized very well. The health screening tent was up early. They had already set up the thin white barricades and porta-johns, and food trucks also arrived early. This was how rally day went.

I put my chair away at around noon, then I went through health screening and received a mask and hand sanitizer. After that, there was the usual walking through the barricades to get to the start of the line. The barricades that were used were the white ones, which seemed to be better as they locked together so people could not cut the line, as there was no yellow tape to sneak under. After this, there was a three-hour wait to go through security, then you could run to the venue and find a seat. At this event, the first three rows were reserved, so I took row four.

Donald Trump came out and said he was "thrilled to be here with hardworking people."

"This is a peaceful protest. We don't call them rallies; we aren't allowed to meet. You are allowed to protest, hence the name, peaceful protest."

It normally takes quite a while to get on the road after a rally due to packed parking lots and congested traffic. I was able to drive half way home and then rested in the car at a hotel parking lot. I normally do that, as it is safer than being in a rest area that is normally in a wooded area.

On September 18, 2020, I watched the Trump rally on television. He spoke in Bedmidji, Minnesota. About ten minutes into his speech on the bottom of the screen, it said Breaking News—Ruth Bader Ginsberg has died.

President Trump walked toward Air Force One with Elton John's "Tiny Dancer" playing in the background, and it was at that time a reporter broke the news. "She just died," Trump said. "I didn't know that; you're telling me now for the first time," he told a reporter. "She led an amazing life; what else can you say? She was an amazing woman; whether you agreed or not, she was an amazing woman who led an amazing life," he said. "I'm sad to hear that."

**Rally #43 – Swanton, Ohio 9/21/2020**

This rally was at the Grand Aire Hanger in Swanton, Ohio. I would go by car to this rally since I was just under a six-hour drive. Upon arrival to the venue area, I noticed the road was blocked off. The line would be right at the blocked off entrance along a busy highway. A short time later, the Jumbotron was set up, which could be viewed while driving down the highway.

Later in the day, more people arrived at check out the venue and see where the line would start. I stayed outside in my sleeping bag. I was able to park my car at a close-by neighbor's large driveway. Later, he put out a sign that said, "Free Parking for Patriots."

I went through the usual health screening, then it was time to head to the venue to find a close seat. Just the first row was reserved, so I sat right behind that and had a perfect view. At this rally, they passed out new signs that said, "Fill That Seat." During the rally, President Trump said he would soon announce a nominee to fill the Supreme Court. The nominee would be announced by the end of the week, and it would be a woman.

This was met with "Fill that seat" chants from the crowd.

## Rally #44 – Middleton, Pennsylvania 9/26/2020

For this trip, I would fly out of Pellston, Michigan. It was a seventy-mile drive to the airport, so I left at 4:00 p.m. It had been many years since I had flown out of this airport. It had been nicely remodeled, and the plane had approximately eighty seats. I then flew to Harrisburg with a short stop in Detroit. This was my easiest arrival yet. The plane landed, I took an escalator downstairs, exited the airport, and walked about one minute to get to the AV Flight Hangar.

By mid-afternoon, people started to getting in line. There was a Fairfield Inn right on the property that some people stayed at. They had a nice restaurant at the hotel. I had a delicious Caesar salad from there.

By 9:00 p.m., I went back to the line to watch the Newport News rally on my phone. It was very noisy outside all night at this rally.

By 3:00 a.m., I decided to leave my chair in line and walk to the wheelchair accessible porta-john, which had yet to be used. I slept in there, which was nice and comfortable, and no noise over there. I should have moved over there sooner. It was great and a clean place to get a little rest before rally day.

This rally was set up like the other: health screening, move into barricades, go through security, then enter venue.

Upon entering the venue, I noticed that the first four rows were reserved, so I went up the side where President Trump entered the stage in the second row.

Just after 5:00 p.m., a big screen TV came on with the nominee announcement from the White House: Supreme Court Justice nominee Amy Coney Barrett. This would be President Trump's third Supreme Court justice nomination in his first term.

After the rally, a large group of us walked over to the hotel restaurant breakfast section and had lots of food to eat that had been ordered.

I walked across the lot to the airport and stayed there for the night. The security opened at 4:30 a.m., so I was able to get to the gated side of the airport.

On the way home, I had a stop in Detroit, so I had lunch at my usual restaurant at this airport, which is Chili's.

## Rally #45 – Duluth, Minnesota 9/30/2020

I headed out to my car just as it became daylight outside for a 7.5-hour drive. I traveled on roads I had never driven before. I thought I would finally reach a highway with two lanes. It was two-way traffic with passing lanes and slow speeds most of the way.

There were no exits for food or gas, but I would continually have to slow down to 35 mph to pass through small towns.

When I arrived at the hangar, the health screening tent was up, and the barricades were being set up. It was a nice sunny day, so I went for a walk across the ariel lift bridge and down by the water to the Duluth North Pier Lighthouse. I decided to eat at Grandma's Saloon, as it was close by, and they have delicious tomato basil soup.

I decided to get a hotel, which was two miles from the hangar, the Country Inn & Suites. I did this so I could watch the debate on television.

At 6:00 a.m., it got busy near the hangar area. There were no cars allowed at this venue; thankfully, I could leave mine at the hotel. So, people had a choice of taking the shuttle from the Amsoil Arena about nine miles away, starting at 11:00 a.m., or people could park their cars at a business, a couple of miles away, and then Lyft back to get in line. I sat on the ground with many other people I had met. They had brought blankets, as it was a very cold day, with rain off and on.

As usual, we went through health screening, then into barricades to form a line and wait for security check. Everything was close by. This time, I got in a bad line to go through the magnetometers. There were only two people ahead of me, but they were pulling things out of their pockets and it ended up taking them ten minutes to get through.

There were a lot of saved rows at this one; row nine was the closest to sit in the center area. I found a third-row seat at the side of the stage where President Trump entered. The backdrop toward the side was a big logging truck. It was a nice setup. Mike Lindell spoke at this rally.

After the rally, we stayed to watch the plane take off. After that, it was off to Applebee's for dinner.

After this rally, I met up with a friend to go to the Green Bay rally. I received a message that Hope Hicks tested positive for COVID, and the rally might end up being canceled. Later that evening, we found out President Trump and Melania Trump had both tested positive for COVID, so all rallies were postponed.

President Trump revealed that he and the first lady had tested positive for coronavirus. "Tonight, @FLOTUS and I tested positive for COVID-19," Mr. Trump tweeted. "We will begin our quarantine and recovery process immediately. We will get through this together."

Emerging from the White House residence at 6:16 p.m., President Trump walked under his own power to his waiting helicopter and displayed no major signs of illness. He was taken to Walter Reed Medical Center, where he would be hospitalized for the next few days.

A short time later, he arrived at the hospital and was seen saluting his military aides. After his arrival, he posted an eighteen-second video to his Twitter account to reassure the American people that he was doing very well after his coronavirus diagnosis. "I want to thank everybody for the tremendous support. I'm going to Walter Reed Hospital. I think I'm doing very well. We're going to make sure things work out. The first lady is doing very well. Thank you very much. I appreciate it. I will never forget it. Thank you."

During his hospital stay, President Trump worked from the presidential offices at Walter Reed. During this time, supporters gathered outside Walter Reed and called for prayers and well wishes as he was being treated.

The Trump campaign sent pizza to supporters that had gathered outside Walter Reed National Military Medical Center.

On Friday evening, just hours after being admitted, President Trump sent White House Chief of Staff Mark Meadows a note to thank supporters who arrived outside. "The president saw you; he said to come out here and thank you all with these chocolates before offering the cheering crowd candy bars."

President Trump's doctor stated he had been administered a Regeneron polyclonal antibody cocktail and had been taking zinc, Vitamin D, famotidine, melatonin, and daily aspirin.

In a video recorded at Walter Reed, President Trump said, "I think we're going to pay a little surprise to some of the great patriots that we have out on the street. They've been out there for a long time, and they've got Trump flags, and they love our country."

A short time later, the presidential motorcade drove by the perimeter of Walter Reed. President Trump was seen waving to his supporters. President Trump continued to improve, and it was stated that he could be discharged that Monday. This is what he tweeted: "I will be leaving the great Walter Reed Medical Center today at 6:30 p.m. Feeling really good. Don't be afraid of covid. Don't let it dominate your life. We have developed, under the Trump Administration, some really great drugs and knowledge. I feel better than I did 20 years ago."

2:37 p.m. October 5, 2020

Upon arriving back at the White House, Trump walked up the staircase of the South Portico entrance and gave the reports standing below a thumbs-up and saluted Marine One.

It was announced that President Trump would hold his first in-person rally since his COVID-19 diagnosis in Central Florida. This rally would take place in Sanford, Florida, at the Sanford International Airport on October 12, 2020.

## Rally #46 – Sanford, Florida 10/12/2020

I immediately made plans as soon as this rally was announced, as I wanted to attend his first rally back since he tested positive for the coronavirus. I would be flying to Orlando, Florida, with a stop in Detroit. There was a thirty-minute delay in Detroit due to a maintenance issue. I went to the venue the day before to scope out the area and see where the line would start.

There would be parking available on site, but not until 8:00 a.m. the next day. About a mile down the road, I saw a canopy set up, not far from some train tracks. There were a few people in line there. I went to the Wawa to get some food and then joined the line for the night.

When traveling by plane, no matter the weather, I would bring a warm coat to lie on or use as a blanket and then have a sweatshirt as a pillow. This worked out great, as you could travel light, as far as bags were concerned, and wear the extra clothes you may need later. The area we slept in was right near the woods, which caused a lot of bugs to fly around in the area.

By 5:00 a.m., there were a lot of cars lined up on the shoulder of the road. As it got closer to move into the parking lot, the people waiting in line without cars just got in with someone to arrive at the venue.

After parking, the line formed near the health screening area, which everyone stayed until 2:00 p.m. The time in line always went by fast, as there were many food trucks and souvenir vendors to look at. It was a nice sunny day to relax in chairs in the line. The supporters that drove to the rallies would bring extra chairs for the people that had flown to use.

It was a nice setup with health screening first. At this one, they did some of the temperature checks first and put a black mark on your wrist, so when they started, the first people in line could go right through to then pick up their wristband, hand sanitizer, and mask.

While going through security, I got behind two extremely slow people, meaning they brought in a lot of items, which slowed my line down. So when this happened, all it meant was that you had to run faster to get to choose an area you liked before those seats were full. I noticed that the first four rows at center stage were reserved, so I chose the second row on the side where President Trump entered the stage.

The venue was packed with thousands of people, as it always was, with many people not able to get in but were able to watch on the Jumbotron set up nearby. It was ninety degrees, but while we waited, we were provided free water and granola bars.

When President Trump's name was announced, the place was electrifying, "He's back!" These grand entrances never got old; it was impossible to describe the electrifying energy in words. It was something that had to be experienced in person to know what was truly happening.

"Hello, Sanford, it's great to be back. That's a lot of people. Sleepy Joe had a rally, and hardly anybody showed up. When you're president of the United States, you can't lock yourself up in a basement. I did more in forty-seven months than Biden did in forty-seven years."

He concluded the rally by thanking everyone for being there, and then, what everyone looks forward to, the playing of "YMCA" with President Trump dancing on stage.

It took about an hour to get out of the lot as there were thousands of cars leaving the venue. Luckily, I found someone to drop me off at the Orlando airport.

Upon arrival at the airport, I printed out my boarding passes that I would need for the following day. I noticed there was a Hyatt Regency in the center of the airport. I decided to use one of my free rooms from hotels.com to stay there.

### Rally #47 – Des Moines, Iowa 10/14/2020

It was my second rally of this trip, which would be at the Des Moines International Airport. After going through security and getting something to drink, I saw a man taking a selfie with the Orlando Sentinel. There was a picture of President Trump with a headline that read, "I feel so powerful." Come, to find out, this man worked for TSA and was also traveling to Des Moines with a stop in Dallas. I noticed he was in the seat next to me. I told him we had a long way to go to DFW, gate E2 to B2, so we did that together along with seven other people that would be working the Des Moines rally. We boarded a tram with multiple stops and then had only thirty minutes to wait until boarding. The plane had to circle before landing as it got caught up in a wind gust. The Des Moines Airport was small and had other hangars that were a bit of a distance from here.

I ended up getting in a taxi to drive around to find the appropriate hangar. When I arrived, the barricades were set up along with the jumbotron. I didn't have anywhere to go at the moment, so I sat under a tree in the shade for the afternoon and watched the Johnstown, Pennsylvania, rally on my phone.

By 7:30, other rally goers arrived, so I joined them. We had a nice dinner at a nearby Perkins and joined the line at 3:00 a.m. There was parking not too far away, but there were shuttles to take you back to the line if you didn't want to walk back.

The health screening started at 10 a.m., then the mazing through barricades to go through security later in the day.

The first few rows at the center stage were reserved, so I decided to be right on the edge to the side where President Trump entered the rally toward the stage.

It was seventy-five degrees with very high winds. It was so windy that one of the barricades was about to blow over. I stood on it until people brought a cement block to hold it down. Everything was secure long before President Trump arrived.

"It's great to be back. Hello, Des Moines. I even brought a hat. Sir, it is so windy out there." We have more enthusiasm now than four years ago."

"Should I take off the tie or not? What do you think?" As the crowd cheered, President Trump loosened his red tie and threw it to the side of the stage. "Oh, that feels so much better. Now we can relax and have a good time"

The next rally was to be held in Macon, Georgia, at the Middle Georgia Regional Airport on October 16, 2020. It was a fifteen-hour drive to Macon from Des Moines. Many supporters would travel from rally to rally, so normally, it was not difficult to catch a ride to the next one.

## Rally #48 – Macon, Georgia 10/16/2020

I found a ride to Macon and was on my way soon after the conclusion of the Des Moines, Iowa, rally. It was a nice drive, and along the way, I listened to the Greenville, North Carolina, rally on the radio.

I arrived at Macon, Georgia, the night before the rally. I joined some other rally goers that had been there scoping out the area. They had secured a parking spot at a nearby residence, where you could see the stage in the distance from the front yard.

I had a nice place to stay outside with many warm blankets. Before going to sleep, I was able to watch the Trump Townhall on my phone.

The line to get in started just after 3:00 a.m. The parking area and shuttles were about three miles away in a grassy lot. We never headed there as we just walked across the street to get in line. The shuttles started to arrive at 10 a.m., and the health screening started after.

After that, we walked through the barricades, which was the line to go through security. Upon entering the venue, the second-row center was available in front of the podium or first row right at the side. I decided to do the side again.

It was a perfect temperature as it was around seventy-five degrees with a slight breeze. We did not see the plane land as it was off to the side. President Trump

THE BEST IS YET TO COME...

noticed us again, as we had been in the same spot for two rallies in a row.

This was a nice setup with many food trucks available. Before the rally, the campaign threw MAGA hats into the crowd. I caught a red one and a camouflage one.

It was an easy exit after the rally as the car was right across the street. About ninety

Minutes later, I was dropped off at the Atlanta airport to fly home the next day.

Upon entering the airport, I was able to print out my boarding passes, but security had closed thirty minutes earlier. They were closed from 11:00 to 4:30 a.m. There were no chairs or benches to sit on. There was a Burger King that was open until 2:30 a.m. I ordered some food but did not find a good place to sit. It was a rough area with people arguing in a very loud manner. These people were not flying out in the morning as they would go in there to hang around instead of being outside all night.

I ended up sitting in the floor of the bathroom to eat peacefully. The staff said I could stay in there as long as I showed them my boarding pass.

After eating, I went upstairs and found a prayer room to lie down in. That lasted about an hour as a staff said I could not stay here as everyone had to be downstairs. So, I went back to the bathroom and stayed there until the airport security opened. It was a nice flight home with a ninety-minute layover in Detroit. As I was in flight from Detroit, large crowds had formed in Muskegon, Michigan, to attend the rally at 5:00 p.m. I was home in time to watch it on RSBN.

This was a great trip. From October 14 to October 17, I was able to take in three rallies in three states. The travel for these needed to be flexible, as I never knew where I would end up and when I would return home as the rallies would pop up while on the road. But I was able to make it work and have a great time doing so.

I waited for the next rallies to be announced to see where I would travel next. My bags were packed, and I was ready to go. At 6:00 p.m. on October 21, I saw the next list of rallies posted. I decided to go to the Villages in Florida. The other choice for that same day was Pensacola, Florida. I purchased my ticket and would be flying to Orlando with a stop in Detroit.

### Rally #49 – The Villages, Florida 10/23/2020

I headed out by plane on October 24. I had trouble getting the movies to load on this flight, so I watched Fox News Live instead; they mainly talked about the laptop scandal.

I arrived at the Villages later in the afternoon. They were setting up for the rally when I arrived. It was neat to see all of the golf carts people rode on, as they were there to check out the venue. Many of them were decorated with Trump signs and merchandise.

I decided to check into a hotel at the Waterfront Inn at the Villages, mainly to watch the debate that evening and have a place to stay as a line would probably not form until morning. It was so nice to go to a restaurant with a buffet, the Golden Coral. In Michigan, there were not a lot of restaurants open.

I got in line at 5 a.m. The line moved a couple of times, and then it was a long way to get to the health screening area to wait in line for entry.

By 9 a.m., everyone was allowed to run through a field and climb a short wooden fence to line up for the day. As time went on, people were brought in by way of golf carts.

For this rally, my name was on the expedited list. So I checked in with identification and received a lanyard to wear. It was a hot day with a lot of standing; at least ten people fainted before getting into the venue.

Since I had expedited entry, my seat was in the bleachers behind the president. There were many sets of bleachers and chairs set up at this rally. It was a good thing as the crowd was enormous. I was at the very top row of the bleachers. This was a great place to view Marine One as it flew in to land not far from the bleachers. It was so exciting to see Marine One fly in overhead; words cannot describe this experience. It was very difficult to video this, as it got extremely windy with sand kicking up in my eyes and face, but I got it!

After this, I moved to the middle area of the bleachers. It was nice to sit here for a change, as I could see the whole crowd. I could even see the words on the teleprompter.

President Trump came onto the stage with an energized crowd as usual. The song that normally played for his grand entrance was "God Bless the USA" by Lee Greenwood. "Thank you, Florida! It's great to be with you and back at the Villages. I see you driving around in those beautiful golf carts. I want to get one."

"If I don't sound like a politician, it's because I'm not a politician. I don't play by the rules of the Washington establishment."

As the rally wound down, I moved to the bottom area of the bleachers close to the stage to see President Trump do the "Happy Dance" as "YMCA" played at the conclusion of the rally. This was one of the most exciting rallies I had ever been to, as there was just so much to take in.

I was dropped off at the Orlando airport after the rally. I had noticed there would be a rally in Lansing, Michigan, coming up. I purchased a ticket to go home.

The Orlando airport was a very comfortable airport to sleep in for the night. They had comfortable couches with outlets nearby for charging. They had restaurants open late, and this was all close to security. In my travels, I noticed that many people would stay the night here as it was so nice, clean, and convenient. My travel home on Delta had the usual layover in Detroit, so once again, I had a meal at Chilis.

On October 24, 2020, President Trump entered the library at about 10:15 to vote. The library was across the street from President Trump's golf course. Supporters had lined the entrance to the polling station and the sidewalk in front of the library, hoping to get a glimpse of the president.

President Trump said he felt more secure voting in person than with a mail-in ballot. "Everything was perfect. Very strict, right by the rules," he said. "When you send in your ballot, it could never be like that, it could never be secure like that."

When asked who he voted for, he said, "I voted for a guy named Trump."

It was now October 26, 2020, the last week of the campaigning for the 2020 election, which was on November 3, 2020. President Trump worked hard by traveling all over the country with multiple daily events. Sometimes an event would be added with only twenty-four hours' notice. And even with such a short notice, people would show up by the thousands. Meanwhile, Joe Biden would have a car rally or a rally with those social distancing circles, and very few would even bother to attend. He spent most of the time in "the basement."

October 26, 2020 to November 3, 2020

I left the house by car on the morning of October 26, knowing I would be heading to Washington Township, Michigan to see a Donald Trump Jr. rally on that evening, and then I would drive to Lansing, Michigan to get in line for President Trump's rally on Tuesday. But, for the rest of the week, I was uncertain as to where I would potentially drive or fly off to next.

This is how the week unfolded. I arrived at Washington Township on Monday afternoon. I was familiar with the venue, as I had seen President Trump speak here in the past. It was a great rally. Donald Trump Jr. spoke for an hour without any notes. After the rally, he came down and spoke to us since we had seats in the front.

## Rally #50 – Lansing, Michigan 10/27/2020

By 9:00 p.m., I was near the front of the line for the Lansing, Michigan, rally the next day. This was a nice setup, as cars could park in the airport lot, and the line to get in was just steps away. Many people slept outside in sleeping bags or tents all night. The health screening was right in front of us, and it was a short maze of barricades to go through to wait to go through security. This was a very fast entry and short walk to the chairs.

The first few rows in the front and center were reserved, so I took a front-row spot on the side right where President Trump walked in. It was a perfect view. The security at this one did not let people push their way to the rail where we were; you could only be up there if you had a seat.

Ted Nugent entertained the crowd while everyone waited for President Trump's arrival. After performing his version of the National Anthem, Ted Nugent said, "God bless real America, God bless the greatest president in our lifetime, Donald Trump."

There was a light rain during most of the rally, but most people were prepared and had disposable rain-coats. The rainy weather did not stop the Trump sup-porters from coming out, as they were there in the thousands. When President Trump took the stage, he stated he was expecting a "great red wave" to roll over Michigan next month.

After the rally, I met up with some other rally goers at a Fazoli's nine miles away. The next rally was not announced yet, so I stayed in the Flint area since I decided to go to a Mike Pence rally on October 28, 2020. The rally was held at the Flint airport. The doors opened at 4:00 p.m. for a 7:00 p.m. start time. The rally was held outdoors with spaced-out chairs. Eventually, the chairs moved up and closer together to allow for more people to stand in the back. I had seen Mike Pence speak at President Trump's rallies, but this was my first time to see him alone.

On October 29, 2020, I drove to the next rally, which would be in Waterford, Michigan, on October 30.

### Rally #51 – Waterford, Michigan 10/30/2020

I arrived at the Oakland County International Airport at noon and received permission to park at a lot of any empty building. There was only room for a few cars here, which would be right across from where the line would start to go in.

There were many gas stations and restaurants in walking distance of the car. It was a little bit cool at night, but not bad at all once I got into my sleeping bag on the ground for the night. Many of us walked over to the Speedway for the most delicious hot chocolate I had ever had.

People gathered during the night, so by the morning, the line to get in was very long. This was another easy entry through security. At this rally, the first five rows were reserved, and the whole side where President Trump walked in was also reserved. I choose to be in row six at the center, which was a very good location for pictures.

This rally had a 2:00 p.m. start time, and we were let into the event before 10:00 a.m., which was nice. President Trump came out to a very enthusiastic crowd with many supporters holding signs, saying, "Four More Years."

After this rally, I noticed that the rest of the rallies for the 2020 campaign were listed on the website. So, I had a plan for the rest of the week, and I would not have to travel out of Michigan. I had some downtime before the next rally, so I decided to spend some time in the Lansing area. I spent a couple of hours at Potter's Park Zoo and then went to see the expanded Horrocks Store. They had some tables set up outside, so I had something to eat there.

### Rally#52 – Washington, Michigan 11/1/2020

I drove the 111 miles to the next rally, which was in Washington, Michigan, at the Michigan Stars Sports Center. I arrived at the venue in the evening and was told to park the car in the field all night. This would be the parking area for tomorrow's rally. The rally was to start at 11:00 a.m. and be the first one of the day.

While waiting in line overnight, many people slept in tents or nearby cars. Some people brought fire pits. I spent most of the night in my sleeping bag under the health screening tent. The screening started early, and by 8:45 a.m., we walked into the building for a security check and then outside to find a seat near the stage. I sat in row five toward the center state. This was a cold rally, thirty-one degrees, with some rain, sleet, and snow.

Ivanka Trump came out and spoke first. President Trump came out wearing a red MAGA hat and a long black coat. While President Trump was on stage, he mentioned the weather a couple of times. "Sir, the wind isn't too strong." "I think it's 50 mph, with a wind chill of negative 20." "I love the people of Michigan; it's worth it."

Right toward the end of the rally, the sun came out and shined right on him; it was an amazing sight to see. It took over an hour to get out of the parking lot, as there were many cars parked in the field, with not many exits to get out. After this rally, I drove 158 miles to Grand Rapids, Michigan, which would be the final stop of the 2020 campaign.

### Rally #53 – Grand Rapids, Michigan 11/2/2020

I was hoping that during my drive to Grand Rapids, my socks and shoes would dry out, but they did not. So, my first stop upon arrival was to purchase some shoes and socks. Then I got some take out at McDonald's. I found a nice place to park for the night, which was the lot right near the small airport office building, which was a part of the Gerald Ford International Airport.

In the morning, cars were allowed to park in a huge field. This was a nice setup, as the cars were right next to the line of chairs going in and close to the many food trucks. It was a nice sunny day, but we were also provided with hand warmers since it was a late-night rally and the temperatures would drop.

The health screening was done later than usual at this event, which was great as the waiting in the line of barricades was only an hour. They had eight magnetometers set up near the line I was in. So, this should have been an easy entry. But, it turned out to be my slowest entry of all. There was one person ahead of me, but what I didn't notice was that it was someone with the media that had a huge backpack full of equipment.

The process of searching this bag took about twenty minutes, and by now, I could not switch to another line. This was unusual, as the media was normally inside long before now. Thankfully, someone had saved me a seat, which was row six center stage. Sometimes, being toward the front of the line means nothing if you pick the wrong line of security. I was fortunate to have only picked a slow line twice of the fifty-six rallies I attended.

This was a busy day on the campaign trail for President Trump. The rallies on November 2, 2020, were as follows: Fayetteville, North Carolina; Scranton, Pennsylvania; Traverse City, Michigan; Kenosha, Wisconsin; and Grand Rapids, Michigan. President Trump was scheduled to take the stage at 10:30 p.m. but was running late since he had such a hectic travel schedule.

There were many speakers at this rally, and many of President Trump's family were in attendance. Mike Pence took the stage at 10:40 p.m.:

Well, hello, Michigan. It is great to be back in the great lake state, just eighty minutes from Election Day, when we re-elect President Donald Trump for four more years. Michigan and America need four more years of President Donald Trump in the White House. In three short years, we made America Great Again. And then 2020 arrived and the coronavirus struck from China.

Right around midnight, President Trump took the stage wearing a red MAGA hat and a long black coat. "God Bless America" was playing while thousands of supporters cheered as he approached the podium for the last speech of the 2020 campaign. "Thank you very much, Grand Rapids! This was our final night prior to a very big victory. And we are going to have another beautiful victory tomorrow. We made history four years ago, and we will make history again tomorrow."

Here are some highlights of the rally:

- ◆ "It would be nice if your governor opened up the state";
- ◆ "Get back to business";
- ◆ "The only one that can roam free is her husband";
- ◆ "We are going to have a great red wave that nobody has ever seen before";
- ◆ "The spied on our campaign, and they got caught";
- ◆ "Look at all that fake news back there";
- ◆ "This is not a crowd of a second-place finisher";
- ◆ "This is the most important election in the history of our country";
- ◆ "From Midland to Mackinac, from Pontiac to Battle Creek, and from Detroit to right here in Grand Rapids, I love Grand Rapids";

- ♦ "We inherit the legacy of American patriots who gave their blood, sweat, and tears to defend our country, our families, and our freedoms";
- ♦ "We stand on the shoulders of American heroes who crossed the oceans, settled the continent, tamed the wilderness, laid down the railroads, raided up the great skyscrapers, won two world wars, defeated fascism and communism, and made America into the single greatest nation in the history of the world";
- ♦ "And the Best is Yet to Come!"
- ♦ "We are returning power to you, the American people"; and
- ♦ "We have made America powerful again, we have made America healthy again, we have made America strong again, we have made America proud again, we have made America safe again, and we will make America great again. Thank you, Michigan, go out and vote."

Wow, what an amazing rally! And just like that, the 2020 election rallies had come to a close, with the final rally being held in my home state of Michigan. It was a very crowded field of cars, which ended up taking me three hours to exit onto the main road.

From here, I headed to the Holiday Inn to sleep for three hours to make the 293-mile trip home. During the drive home, I thought about the previous week. It sure was a busy one. The week started with a Donald Trump Jr. rally, also one Mike Pence rally, and four President Trump rallies. I arrived home early in the afternoon, unpacked, and repacked for a trip the day after Election Day.

Election night had finally arrived. The night many of us had been waiting for, November 3, 2020, the night President Donald Trump would be re-elected. I was glued to the television, just like in 2016. But, this time, I was not worried, as I was confident that he would win.

From January 2020 through November 2, 2020, I had attended twenty-two Trump rallies. The crowds were huge, and the message was positive. As I watched, the results looked good. President Trump led in all the battleground states by large margins. I decided to get about two hours rest, as in the morning, I had a 297-mile drive to the airport.

When I woke up, I was surprised to see what had happened and was unsure as to what went on. These were the headlines and statements I saw online:

- ◆ "Arizona is still in play";
- ◆ " Arizona & Pennsylvania equal re-election";
- ◆ "There is a pathway to victory";
- ◆ "Wisconsin has more votes than people living in Wisconsin"; and
- ◆ "Ballots showed up out of nowhere at 3:00 a.m."

President Trump was winning in Michigan and Wisconsin by a solid lead; the vote count paused, then Biden jumped up by 200,000 in Michigan overnight without adding a single vote to Trump or third-party candidates. We had witnessed an attempt to steal the presidential election. The minute it was clear that President Trump would win, the counting stopped. If the media was honest, they would have called North Carolina, Georgia, Michigan, and Pennsylvania. President Trump had enough real votes to win each of these states. But, when it was clear he would win, they stopped the counting.

There was chaos in Detroit, as workers blocked windows and bar observers. There were mail-in ballots in Pennsylvania that were accepted after the deadline. This could equate to hundreds of thousands of ballots.

The Democrats did every trick in the book to obstruct poll watchers. They denied access, blocking poll watchers from seeing the voter lists, shut down elevators, chained exit doors shut, told new volunteers to leave as they arrived, and prohibited volunteers from returning once they left.

The most important issue was probably the Dominion software. There were whistleblowers coming forward and analyses being done. It was very likely that millions of ballots were flipped from Trump to Biden. After catching up on all of the news, it was time to drive to the Flint airport.

I had decided to go on a relaxing trip to Myrtle Beach right after the election. I spent several days at Breaker's Resort, which is right on the ocean. While away, I did not watch the news, as it was all so negative. I remember on the morning that I was to fly home, I thought, "What if I just stayed here?" It was a nice escape from the election news and all the negativity that surrounded it.

Upon returning home, I saw many "Stop the Steal" rallies popping up all over the county. On November 21, 2020, hundreds of Trump supporters gathered in Atlanta in front of the Capitol building. Later that evening, they had another rally in front of the Governor's Mansion. It was claimed that President Trump lost the election due to massive voter fraud.

Similar demonstrations were held in other states, demanding more time to recount the election results and investigate fraud. Trump supporters held a "Stop the Steal" rally in Lansing, as Michigan was preparing to certify the November 3rd vote.

Hundreds of supporters gathered in Phoenix in an effort to ensure the integrity and transparency of the November 3rd election results. I did not know how all of this would go. But, I did know that the election was **stolen and rigged**. **Trump won**! I know it, you know it, and everybody knows it.

It was announced that President Trump would hold a rally in Valdosta, Georgia, ahead of the runoff elections in two Senate races. Senator David Perdue and Senator Kelly Loeffler were expected to be in attendance.

### Rally #54 – Valdosta, Georgia 12/5/2020

I flew to Atlanta the day before the rally. Another rally goer passing through picked me up in Atlanta for a 220-mile ride to Valdosta. A resident that lived close to the venue charged fifteen dollars per car, so we had a nice close place to park.

We had a delicious meal at Fazoli's before starting a line of chairs. It was raining off and on and had turned cold. Some stayed in cars, chairs, or under the health screening tent. I lay on the health screening table for a while. It was not very comfortable, so I decided to sleep on the floor of an unused porta john. It was much warmer in there and just steps away from the line.

After going through security, I was able to find a good seat on the side of the stage. This rally was mainly a rally to get out the vote for Loeffler and Perdue. Melanie Trump spoke at this rally. "It is my pleasure to welcome the president of the United States, Donald J. Trump." President

Trump began by wishing everyone a Merry Christmas. "This election was rigged, and we can't let it happen again. I won all the swing states by a lot."

After the rally, I got dropped off at the airport in Atlanta and was home by early afternoon the following day.

It was announced there would be a March for Trump event in Washington, DC, on December 12, 2020. I decided to go since I had not attended any of the "Stop the Steal" events. I left the day before the event. I flew to Washington, DC, with a stop in Detroit. I landed in DC before noon and got an early check-in at Harrington's Hotel.

It was a nice sunny day, sixty-five degrees. I walked near the White House to see the Christmas trees on display. There was one real large one and fifty small ones that represented each state. I spent the whole afternoon walking around outside just sight- seeing. Later in the evening, I had a delicious Caesar salad for dinner at Trump International.

I headed out early in the morning to listen to General Michael Flynn speak outside in front of the Supreme Court Building. After that, I headed to Freedom Plaza. Just as I arrived, President Trump's helicopter flew over, as he was on his way to the Army vs. Navy game in New York.

Mike Lindell was one of the speakers on the stage at Freedom Plaza. He explained there was an algorithm set in the Dominion voting machines to switch a percent of Trump votes to Biden. They realized they did not cheat at a high enough rate, so they stopped counting and pulled out suitcases of ballots. Later in the evening, there was a "Stop the Steal" rally in front of the J. W. Marriott.

That Sunday, I went to the "Keep Christmas" rally. Mike Lindell spoke here along with many other speakers. They also had some nice Christmas music playing.

My flight out of DC left thirty minutes late, delayed, as it had to be cleaned. I landed in Minneapolis at 7:35 p.m., and my plane boarded at 7:40 p.m. It was a long walk in Minneapolis, as I always land and have to go from one end of the airport to the other. Luckily, I made it and had one minute to spare.

It was announced that President Trump would hold a campaign rally in Dalton, Georgia, on January 4, 2021. This was to show support for two Republican senators, Kelly Loeffler and David Perdue.

## Rally #55 – Dalton, Georgia 1/4/2021

This was a very snowy three-hour drive to the airport in Saginaw, Michigan. They had a storm during the night, and many of the side roads I traveled on were not plowed. It was very slippery and hard to keep the car on the road. I boarded the plane, which had a stop in Detroit, to land in Atlanta.

I got here much earlier than I had planned because two of my previous flights were changed to earlier flights. I had a lot of time to look around the Atlanta airport to find a place to sleep for the night. I walked around the D terminal and found that D 14 had larger chairs that did not have armrests in the way when lying down. I had my dinner at Famous Famiglio Pizza.

By 11:00 p.m., I met up with another rally goer. In the morning, we took a shuttle to the rental car area. We were now on our way to Dalton, Georgia. We had heard about an event that was early in the day. So, we decided to go to it. It was a "Save the Senate" rally at Cherokee Brewing Pizza Company with Kristi Noem as the speaker. After this event, we headed to check out the venue for the Trump rally the next day.

There were a couple of nearby residents that were allowing parking. This was nice, as the vehicles would be in walking distance to the line going into the rally. We were allowed to line up right at the gate. Some people stayed in their cars for the night. I had borrowed a sleeping bag and staying in line outside.

It was a very cold night. In the morning, the sleeping bags were covered in frost. The sun came out during the day, and it warmed up.

Upon entering the venue, I decided to take the side stage a couple of rows back. This was another "Save the Senate" rally. President Trump said, "By the way, there's no way I lost Georgia." "When you win in a landslide and it's rigged, it's not acceptable."

While I sat in my chair, waiting for the rally to start, I knew I had made the wrong decision about the January 6, 2021, "Save America" rally. I had not planned to attend the rally, as I had a flight home the next day. But, seeing a lot of my friends there, and knowing they would all go, I decided to cancel my flight home and catch a ride to Washington, DC. I wanted to be there to attend the "Save America" rally and listen to what the many speakers had to say.

# Chapter 7

# Save America Rally – January 6, 2021

──── ★ ────

### Rally #56 – The Ellipse at White House 1/6/2021

After the Dalton rally, we were off to Washington, DC, which was a nine-hour drive. We stopped along the way for food and snacks because most of the restaurants in DC were closed. While in DC, we stayed at the Comfort Inn. At around midnight, we headed out with everything we needed for the following day. When we arrived at the Ellipse, a line of about twenty people had already formed. We got in line with our chairs for the night.

By 7:00 a.m., the line moved into the maze of barricades and straight through to screening and security. At this venue, all the seats by the stage and way back were all VIP. Then there was a smaller area in front of the media that was for general admission.

Many speakers took the stage before President Trump spoke. President Trump took the stage and asked the fake news media to show the crowds. There were thousands of people in attendance, which went way back past the Washington Monument. "The media is the biggest single problem we have, and this year, they rigged an election. We will never give up, we will never concede; it doesn't happen. You don't concede when there's theft involved. We will 'Stop the Steal.' Does anybody believe that Joe had 80 million votes?"

If Mike Pence does the right thing, we win the election. We are gathered together in the heart of our nation's capital for one very basic and simple reason, to save our democracy. We don't have a free and fair press. And it's become the enemy of the people. I know that everyone here will soon be marching over to the Capitol Building to peacefully and patriotically make your voices heard. My fellow American, for our children and for our beloved country, and I say this despite all that has happened, the Best is Yet to Come!

So, we are going to walk down Pennsylvania Avenue. I love Pennsylvania Avenue, and we're going to the Capitol; we're going to try and give our Republicans the kind of pride and boldness they need to take back our country. Let's walk down Pennsylvania Avenue. I want to thank you all, and God bless America.

After the "Save America" rally, we walked the 1.7 miles toward the Capitol Building. It took a long time to get there as there were thousands of people walking in the streets. It seemed that people were getting angry as they walked, as they heard that Mike Pence would not do the right thing.

It was very crowded as we approached the Capitol Building area, so we ended up quite a distance from it, on the back side. I did not see any violence from back there. It was peaceful and patriotic, with people singing and waving flags.

After we were there a while, we went up a sideways barricade to get on a platform to take some pictures of the crowd that flowed to the Washington Monument. We did not stay in that area long. We went back down to our original spot. It wasn't long, and President Trump put out a video announcement, telling supporters to go home and go home in peace.

At this time, we decided to walk back to the hotel, as from where we were, there was nothing going on, just people standing around. When we got back to the hotel and turned on the television, I was surprised to see people walking around inside the Capitol Building. We did not have cell phone service, so we had not received updates.

Early the next morning, I took a Lyft to the airport. I had attended my fifty-sixth Trump rally, and that's where my book would end. I would eventually write a book about attending fifty-six Trump rallies in twenty different states and highlight the news cycle.

But, in the middle of July, something horrible happened. It motivated me to write my book and tell the truth about what really happened.

# Chapter 8

# Hit Piece

— ★ —

In the middle of July 2021, I became a victim of a hit piece written by a third-rate reporter. I received messages and calls from friends telling me about the statements online that I supposedly said. These statements were untrue and very damaging. A book had come out on Amazon, which was full of lies. The author used two statements that I did not say to promote book sales. Here are the statements:

"We were just there to overthrow the government."

"We were supposed to be fighting until the end."

Wow! How horrible. I never said these things, as I was there to watch the "Save America" rally.

I had ordered this book, so when it came out, I had wondered what else was in it. I was shocked to see my full name, workplace, hometown, and the car I drive printed in this book. I would never have agreed to any of that. And the worst part was, as I read it, I discovered many untruths. Here are some examples:

After the rally in Battle Creek, Michigan, in December 2019, the author said that I went to a Denny's for breakfast with friends and said, "Look, here's a picture of us in line."

First of all, I have never been to a Denny's in Michigan, and the friend he is talking about drove home after the rally.

In spring 2020, I was told that some Trump supporters would do a virtual online Zoom. I was off work that day and choose not to participate. But, of course, this is what he said about me. "Saundra didn't make it. She had been crushing overtime shifts at Wal-Mart, trying to restock aisles of toilet paper and hand sanitizer that panicked shoppers had depleted." Obviously, we all know that this is not true. If the reporter researched this topic, he would know that the stores did not have paper products to stock and rarely received hand sanitizer. How can items be stocked when they do not exist? And all of a sudden, I was working in a department I had never worked in before. My name should not have been mentioned during the Zoom topic. I did not participate, end of story. But, no, someone had to insert statements that did not happen.

It was June 2020, and I was in Tulsa. It was the morning of the rally, and we were getting ready for a longer-than-usual run in the heat to the venue. It would be a run of just under a mile. And this is what the author said about me: "She was in pain, and the block felt more like a mile." This is insignificant but not true. We ran many blocks all through town to get from the health screening to the venue. I put these insignificant statements here so it can be seen that to a reporter, no lie is too small. They will add colorful statements to keep the book more interesting, I suppose?

# Chapter 9

## Enemy of the People

———— ★ ————

How did this happen? I have been asking myself that very question, and this is what I came up with. This reporter infiltrated into a group of Trump supporters that attended rallies on a regular basis. I believe it started some time in 2019. He wrote some nice articles about them a few times. He was now thought of as a "good guy." I was not at any of those rallies. I was given his number to call him. When I did, he just asked a few questions about rallies, and it was not a big deal.

In January 2021, he called to ask me my experience on January 6. I told him that I went to the "Save America" rally, then walked to the back of the Capitol Building. My friends and I were way at the back and did not see any violence. For us, it was a patriotic event with many people singing and waving flags.

At one point, we climbed up a small barricade to then get some pictures of the large crowd surrounding the Washington Monument. We then returned to our standing spot at the back of the Capitol Building. After hearing President Trump's message stating for people to go home, we walked back to the hotel. I then said I was surprised to see so many people walking around inside the Capitol, as I did not know that had happened.

Thinking back on that phone conversation now, I remember him being disappointed, as my story was boring. He didn't seem to like the fact that I had no idea people were walking around inside the Capitol Building, and conveniently left that statement out of the book: "I said we didn't go there to steal anything or do any damage."

So, here is what the fake news media does, right here, they insert a line, which I **never** said: "We were just there to overthrow the government." Who says something like that? Certainly not me. Who added that statement? Was it the reporter or the publisher? And why did they do it? This is very dangerous behavior.

"They" added a line that was not said by me, which caused me threats online and hate mail sent to my home address. I took my social media down, as I was not able to sleep at night or even function during the day. The Twitter comments were the worst ones:

"You are a terrorist."
"You are going to prison."

What happened was other news outlets said, "Trump supporter storms Capitol and was only there to overthrow the government, listing my name. If they read the book, it does state that I am one hundred yards from the Capitol Building. But, no one read that part. The media outlets did not even investigate what they were reporting on; it was terrible.

The reporter was eventually told that I was furious and did not like the book. On July 18, 2021, the reporter called me. I did not answer. He texted me, stating that he was sorry he missed me and was eager to talk to me to understand what was going on. He wanted me to call him back. I texted back, stating that I did not trust him and to please leave me alone, as I never wanted to hear from him again. The next text stated that he thought I would like the book and was crushed that I did not. He wanted to know what he could do to help. I told him the damage was already done, and this is where we part ways.

I was shocked by his texts. He thought I would like the book. What was there to like? It was a hit piece on me and the greatest president of all time, Donald J. Trump.

How can he help? First of all, you tell me you are writing a book. Secondly, you let people in this book know that their personal information will be in it. I would have never spoken to him, as I would never want my name in this sort of book.

Thinking back to before Donald Trump was president, if I saw something on TV or in the newspaper, I thought it was true. "I saw it on television, so therefore, it is true." I think that President Trump's single greatest accomplishment is exposing the fake news media. If it wasn't for him, I would probably still believe that what they say is true because I did not know any better.

The reason I am talking about this hit piece and the fake news media is to let people know how easily this can happen to anyone. They omit a couple of statements that you make and insert something else to change the whole meaning of what really happened.

This cannot continue, and it needs to stop now before an innocent person is seriously injured. The general public might belief the untruths they see in print and react to them in a harmful way on an innocent person.

If you are reading this book, I am asking you to be very careful when talking to reporters. I do not want what happened to me to happen to anyone else. My beliefs are that you do not put names of unknown citizens of the general public in a book without their approval. And you should never put their personal information in a book when you know it could be damaging and harmful.

I am not here to put the reporter's name or workplace in my book because I then would be stooping to his level. We should pray for this reporter and the rest of the fake news media; that they see the light and be more careful with their wording. They need to go back to just reporting the facts instead of reporting what they want us to believe. When I first saw the statement, the "media is the enemy of the people," I did not give it much thought. But, now that I have experienced it firsthand, they truly are.

# Chapter 10

## Trump 2024

★

The question of the hour: will Donald Trump run in 2024? Originally, I thought he would wait and decide after the 2022 election. But, after hearing a Sean Hannity interview, my guess is that he will run again. Sean Hannity asked Donald Trump, without giving the answer, "Have you made up your mind?" "Yes," Trump said. So, he has made up his mind, and I am hoping that he does.

At CPAC in 2021, President Trump easily won the straw poll. This is a poll where attendees are asked who they would like to see run for the White House in 2024. President Trump has effectively frozen the field more than three years before the next election.

He is the best candidate for the job. He made America great again during his first term. And if he is elected in 2024, he will "Make America Great Again" again. So, with that being said, "The Best Is Yet to Come."

# Chapter 11

# Trump Properties

——— ★ ———

am grateful to have had the pleasure of visiting some of the Trump properties.

**Trump International Hotel Las Vegas**

This is a sixty-four-story hotel located on Fashion Show Drive. It opened on March 31, 2008. It has two restaurants and 1,282 rooms. The location is great as it is walking distance to the Fashion Show Mall. They also have a nice pool and eatery. Some people stay at this non-gaming hotel to avoid the extra noise and crowds.

**Trump International Washington, DC**

This hotel was the site of the Old Post Office and Clock Tower, located on 1100 Pennsylvania Avenue. The hotel's grand opening was celebrated on October 26, 2016. This hotel has a beautiful lobby and restaurant area. It attracts locals and travelers, as it is a great place to meet for a delicious meal. It has the largest luxury hotel ballroom in the city. The hotel offers 263 luxurious guest rooms and suites, of which no two are identical.

## Trump International New York

This hotel is located at 1 Central Park West and is one of the most luxurious hotels overlooking Central Park. The 176-room hotel has rooms with floor to ceiling windows, two restaurants, a terrace, and an indoor pool. I really enjoyed my stay here, as it was in a great location to just walk outside and do some sightseeing; the rooms had doorbells, and you never knew what kind of treat was waiting on the other side. One time, I received a delicious box of chocolates.

## Trump Tower

Trump Tower is located at 721 5th Avenue between 56th and 57th Street. It has fifty-eight floors and is 664 feet tall. It serves as headquarters for the Trump Organization.

I remember being so excited to finally eat one of the delicious taco bowls at Trump Grill. I have eaten there many times, and the food and service are always excellent. I would highly recommend eating here if you get the chance. It has such a nice atmosphere. They also have a Trump Café, Trump Ice cream Parlor, and two Trump stores.

## Trump International Golf Links & Hotel Doonbeg

This luxury oceanfront hotel is situated in a small village on the corner of Ireland's southwest coast, in scenic

County Clare. It includes fine dining, a spa, and a beautiful golf course. I really enjoyed my time here.

As you approach the hotel, you go down a long winding road, basically in the middle of nowhere. The hotel consists of 218 hotel suites that are spread out in many different buildings. Upon entering the room, you will find a delicious box of chocolates. I later found out that they were made onsite.

I spent most of my time outside taking in the beautiful view, walking along the ocean, and collecting sea shells. There was an amazing salt-like smell in the air that was indescribable. The golf course looked beautiful with a big clock, similar to the one out front at Trump Tower in New York.

## Mar-a-Lago

And last but not least is the beautiful Mar-a-Lago. Mar-a-Lago is a resort and national historic landmark in Palm Beach, Florida. The Atlantic Ocean is to the east, and Florida's Intracoastal Waterway is to the west.

The first time I saw the inside of Mar-a-Lago was in March 2021. It was so exciting to finally see it in person, as I had heard so much about this property. It has an eye-catching gate to enter through, and once inside, the landscaping is something you don't see every day. There is a large pool, which is the center of where many outdoor events take place. Mar-a-Lago is such beautiful and peaceful place to be. The feeling you have while there can not be described in words. Everyone needs to visit here at least once to experience the peaceful existence.

# Acknowledgments

——— ★ ———

Firsst of all, I want to thank my family and friends for supporting me on this journey. I also want to thank the many Trump supporters I have met from all over the world. There are too many to name, but you know who you are. I now have many new friendships that will last a lifetime. Thank you to the many local citizens that showed up at the line to provide us with food, water, pop, blankets, pillows, hand warmers, raincoats, and anything else that was needed.

Just recently, I went through my twenty large binders of notes. I knew that someday I would attempt to write a book. In doing this, I was reminded of so many events that had taken place over the years.

In 2016, I observed how Donald Trump reacted with people. It was an exciting time, especially when he would do the "rope line." The anticipation and excitement was like nothing I had ever seen before. He would go down the line and take selfies, autographs, and visit with people. He would take time for everyone.

During this time, I obtained several autographs and spoke to him many times. Donald J. Trump was running for president of the United Sates, but he was one of us.

A person for "We the People." He was not a politician; he was a friend to all people.

Back in 2016, when the venue would occasionally hold only 1200 people, Trump would call people out, "There's my guy." He would always take the time to acknowledge people he recognized in the crowd. And when this happened, it was always a special moment.

So, thank you, President Trump, for being a president for all people. Thank you for your many accomplishments: securing the border, defeating ISIS, eliminating the Obama Care mandate, tax cuts, reducing regulations, record 401ks and stock market numbers, lowering prescription drug prices, the First Step Act, passed Right to Try, brought factories and industries back, support for American Farmers, Veterans Affairs Accountability Act, created the world's most prosperous economy, lowest unemployment rate, fair and reciprocal trade, America First policies, and American energy independence, just to name a few.

Thank you, President Trump, for giving me confidence to stand up for myself and not be afraid. Thank you, President Trump, for giving me the determination to write a book. Twelve days and ninety hours later, this book was written.

You have made America wealthy again, you have made America strong again, you have made America proud again, you have made America safe again, and you will "Make America Great Again" again!

Thank you, my friend, President Donald J. Trump. The Best is Yet to Come...

CPSIA information can be obtained
at www.ICGtesting.com
Printed in the USA
LVHW010036200122
708966LV00008B/160

9 781662 838323